Christianity and Reincarnation

Rudolf Frieling

Christianity and Reincarnation

Floris Books

Translated by Rudolf and Margaret Koehler

First published in English by Floris Books in 1977
Originally published in German under the title
Christentum und Wiederverkörperung by Verlag Urachhaus

ISBN 0 903540 05 3

Printed in Great Britain
by R & R Clark, Edinburgh

Contents

Introduction

A twofold tendency is particularly noticeable in people's view of life at the present time. On the one hand there is an increase in a materialistic outlook which denies any supersensible reality—even in Christian theology. A striking example of this is the doctrine of 'Total Death' whereby the human soul is denied any individual metaphysical existence; death ends everything until the Last Day. In between there is nothing. Earlier religious philosophy is destroyed by the process of 'demythologizing'. On the other hand, as a result, a far-eastern spirituality invades this religious vacuum, offering a new content to meet the feeling of spiritual hunger.

Faced with all this, it is time Christianity pondered its essential nature, to which justice cannot be done either by a materialistic outlook or by an old Indian wisdom.

In what follows the attempt is made to show how Christianity, if conscious of its own spiritual foundations, can encounter not only materialism but also eastern philosophy with a superior life philosophy of its own. This will be explained especially in relation to the idea of reincarnation, which is often regarded as the domain of Indian philosophy. The idea of reincarnation can be seen in an entirely new light in connection with the Christian hope that the unique and basic mystery of the Resurrection of Christ will bring about a 'resurrection on the last day' for all mankind. It was first seen in this light in Rudolf Steiner's Anthroposophy. In what follows we hope to show not only how the idea of reincarnation in its anthroposophical form can fit into the Christian outlook without contradiction, but even how it satisfactorily completes it.

It will be necessary to direct our attention first to the fact of Christ's existence, which is basic for all Christianity. Then it will be seen that the idea of reincarnation, though not applicable to Christ Himself, is all the more so to mankind's becoming Christian, which should follow from Christ's becoming Man.

What happens to the individual between his death and the Last Day? Theology has occasionally felt the existence of an 'eschatological gap' in the whole Christian outlook. Finally we shall examine the sayings in the Bible which are, or seem to be, related to the idea of reincarnation, and furthermore consider especially the eschatological-apocalyptic parts of the New Testament. If considerable space is allowed for describing what belongs essentially to Christianity, it is with the intention of dealing with the relationship of Christianity and reincarnation not only peripherally but as far as possible *ex fundamento*—which means from the point of view of the Resurrection.

It should be added that in The Christian Community, to whose theologians the author belongs, reincarnation is not taught as a dogma.

Christianity and Reincarnation

The Norwegian saga* tells how King Olaf the Saint (995–1029) once rode with his retainers past the grave mound of the good King Geirstaderalf. One of the company asks the king:—'Tell me, Lord, is it you that lies buried here?' The king answered: 'My spirit never had two bodies and it never will have, either now or on the Day of Resurrection. If I ever said anything different, the right faith was not in me.' Then his follower said: 'It is what people say—that once, passing this place, you said, "Here I was and here I rode".' The king answered: 'That I never said, and may I never say so.' Whereupon great excitement came over the king; he spurred his horse and hurried away from that place.—

This scene shows that the opinion that man lives more than once on earth is by no means merely an Indian doctrine. It was also known to men before Christianity outside the Far East, even in Northern Europe. The Olaf story is symptomatic of the relationship between traditional Christian belief and the idea of reincarnation. The newly converted Christian, Olaf, vigorously rejects the old idea which he has apparently shared. He no longer wants to know anything about it. The manner in which he rejects it, however, is striking. The strong emotion of the king could lead one to suppose that he has not yet inwardly finished with the whole matter. This example enables one to divine how the newly accepted Roman Catholic Christianity violently thrusts aside old traditions and feelings, not without revealing the unmastered remains of those feelings. An example of this can also be found in the Edda.† At the end of the second song, the one who hands down the songs of Helge Hunding's Bane remarks that the return of men to earth was a belief of the past, but is now considered an old wives' tale. One cannot fail to sense a certain note of regret. Here, too, is the apparently

* Flateyjarbók, Vol. II, P. T. Malling, Christiania, 1862. Cited by Emil Bock, *Wiederholte Erdenleben*, Verlag Urachhaus, Stuttgart, 1952, p. 16.

† Compare Emil Bock, *Wiederholte Erdenleben*, p. 15.

inevitable bidding farewell to old traditions which is the consequence of Christianization. It looks as if Christianity and the idea of reincarnation could not coexist.

In the history of Christian dogma there is nowhere any mention of reincarnation. Only once it almost happened that reincarnation was drawn into Christian thinking. Origen (d. 254) talks about the existence of human souls before birth, about previous formative activities, the consequences of which are brought into earthly incarnation, showing positive or negative effects. On the basis, however, of texts and fragments of texts that have come down to us it cannot be clearly established whether in Origen's opinion such pre-birth existences are lived here on earth or on different levels of existence in the universe. But in any case, Origen, as a Christian thinker, does teach pre-existence. The soul does not come into existence only with the body; at the moment of incarnation it already has a history behind it. Pre-existence, as Origen sees it, has without doubt a most definite content. Entry into earth existence is not unconditioned; '*antiquiores causae*', causes from the past, work into it. Origen distinguishes in the soul between a spiritual nucleus as the very bearer of the individuality, and a part that makes a link with the body.

If pre-existence is questioned, then any possibility of reincarnation is done away with. Three hundred years after Origen, the teaching of pre-existence was officially condemned in the Christian Church, in 543 at Constantinople; probably this condemnation was reaffirmed at the Fifth Ecumenical Council in the Hagia Sophia in 553. The relevant formulation reads: *Si quis fabulosam animarum praeexistentiam et quae ex illis consequitur: monstruosam restitutionem* (*apokatastasin*) *assuerit, anathema sit.* (If anyone should asseverate the fabulous idea of the pre-existence of souls and anything following therefrom, namely the monstrous idea of restitution (*apokatastasis*), be he anathema.) Thus pre-existence is banished to the realm of heathen tales. As a 'consequence' there appears not reincarnation but 'apokatastasis', the final restoration and bringing back of the soul into the divine. This thought, which for Origen followed from repeated existences, is called not only 'fabulous' but even 'monstrous'. Perhaps they would have found an even stronger word of rejection had Origen taken these various forms of existence as reincarnations on earth.

Therewith any possibility of reincarnation was eliminated from official Christian teaching. In Roman Catholicism, 'Creationism' came to the fore: each time at the beginning of an individual life, God creates out of nothing a new soul for the body that is coming into being. Protestantism was more inclined to adopt 'Traducianism': the soul is produced together with the body as an offspring of the parental substance. According to Creationism, the soul still has a supersensible reality to be distinguished from the body, while Traducianism promotes the materialistic doctrine of the inseparability of the body-soul unit, an idea now increasingly accepted, even by theologians.

Wherever the idea of reincarnation appeared in western philosophy in the eighteenth, nineteenth and twentieth centuries, it was outside ecclesiastical Christianity, in connection with traditions of the ancient mysteries, or stimulated through the discovery of Indian philosophy, or even in the form of personal feelings and divinations. In his book *Wiederholte Erdenleben* (Repeated Earth Lives), Emil Bock gives an astonishing number of quotations. The Anthroposophy of Rudolf Steiner (1861–1925) takes an entirely different position. Here reincarnation becomes evident as the result of spiritual investigation carried out in a way possible for modern consciousness. The nature of that anthroposophical concept of reincarnation will concern us in what follows. It is rejected by church theology, even definitely opposed. It was taken seriously and acknowledged especially from the Christian point of view almost alone in contemporary Christianity by the theologians of The Christian Community, which came into being in 1922.* They are convinced that the present hour in world evolution demands that, after so many centuries of disregard and neglect of the idea of reincarnation, the matter is taken up again and the 'Christianity and Reincarnation' problem approached anew.

First of all we turn to the question of the essence of Christianity.

* Friedrich Rittelmeyer, *Wiederverkörperung*, Stuttgart, 1931 (*Reincarnation*, London, *c.* 1931, undated); Emil Bock, *Wiederholte Erdenleben*, first edition, Stuttgart, 1932.

I

Christianity

Fact and Doctrine

'Christ is not the teacher, as one is wont to say, Christ is not the inaugurator, He is the *content* of Christianity.' These words of Schelling in the twenty-fifth lecture of his *Philosophie der Offenbarung* (Philosophy of Revelation) may be taken as a classic expression of how one could say Christianity views itself.

In modern times people have become accustomed to regard Christianity as one of the great world religions whose inaugurator, if not the Rabbi Jesus of Nazareth, could then perhaps be held to be St. Paul. The rites and doctrines of early Christianity are compared with the religious environment of late Judaism and the mystery cults of the Hellenistic world. Correspondences, relationships, similarities are found. The discoveries at Qumran have even raised the question whether Qumran should be taken as the real cradle of Christianity. The 'originality' of Christianity is questioned.

Adolf Holl* puts it as follows: 'But what was original in him [Jesus]?' It looks as if Christianity has to give up the claim to 'originality' in face of this investigation into its early environment by religious historians. On the other hand, Adolf Holl feels that such an analysis of Christianity into various environmental elements does not do justice to it as an actual historical fact. Has something perhaps been overlooked in this estimation? He continues: 'It has been said, and perhaps rightly, that the actual doctrines that Jesus preached were not always

* *Jesus in bad company*, Collins, London, 1972, pp. 33, 34.

original. That means, then, that we shall not be able to answer the question of the nature of Jesus's originality scientifically . . . If we cannot analyse Jesus's originality scientifically (which is not to say that it is not fact), this does not prevent us from further reflections on this theme.' Certainly not. Further reflection could lead to the question whether a different way of knowing should be sought, better suited to the subject, since analysis, the resolution into single elements, apparently fails to come to terms with the matter. 'Which is not to say that it [the originality] is not fact . . .' This is indeed a significant statement.

To the criticism of the analytical-scientific method, which is obviously not helpful in this field, may be added a statement made already in an essay in 1928 by the Protestant Church historian, Karl Holl:* 'Especially when one starts analysing Christianity, what seems to me an imperative question arises: What is it that made Christianity gain the victory over all other religions? I regard it as the gravest omission that current research in the history of religion absolutely ignores this simple question. . . . Yet it is a fact obvious to everyone not only that in the end Christianity alone always held its ground, but that its confessors always felt themselves to be different from adherents of other religions. There must be some reason for this.' Like Adolf Holl, Karl Holl also speaks here about a 'fact' which has apparently escaped scientific attention.

In 1902 a book was published with the title: *Das Christentum als mystische Tatsache* (Christianity as Mystical Fact). It was not written by a theologian, but by Rudolf Steiner, the founder of Anthroposophy. It takes its place exactly where Adolf Holl and Karl Holl indicate the failure of the scientific approach. By means of a modern spiritual research, Rudolf Steiner gave from 1902 till 1925 a comprehensive description of Christianity that fully recognizes this factual character. Schelling's intuition was thereby reconfirmed in a new way: Christ is not so much a teacher and founder as—in an absolutely exact sense—the content of Christianity. The fully justified question about His 'originality' could then be answered in this way: that which was new in what Christ brought was Himself—in the strict sense of the words, *He Himself.* Yet this may only be said if the

* Quoted by H. Zahrut, *Es begann mit Jesus von Nazareth*, Gütersloher Verlagshaus, 1969, p. 66.

existence of higher planes of supersensible facts and supersensible individual beings is recognized. A thorough study of Rudolf Steiner's path of knowledge can lead to such a recognition. Thereby it can become evident that the powerful impact that the rise of Christianity undeniably made upon the history of mankind came about through the fact that at the turning point of history a being of highest rank entered the realm of man on earth.

This entry occurs through the actual event of Golgotha, which includes the Death and Resurrection. The Risen One can say: 'I am with you always, to the close of the age' (Matt.28:20). In view of this, the preceding events, the teaching and healing of the Rabbi Jesus, have the character of mere preparation. In the Gospels themselves it becomes evident that this Rabbi Jesus consciously went towards a decisive event and endeavoured to awaken in His disciples a divination of that forthcoming event which would be 'the actual deed' in comparison with the preceding deeds which were just 'signs'. When, after their enlightenment and inspiration at Pentecost, the disciples had found the power to bear witness to their experience, they did not speak at first about the doctrines and deeds of the Rabbi Jesus but about the change through which their master had gone by dying and rising from death. Right at the beginning of Christianity there stands this pointer to a fact. It was an historical fact—'under Pontius Pilate'—as well as a mystical one, which means that spiritual powers from higher realms had been at work. St. Paul has declared that without this fact the apostolic message would be nothing (1Cor.15:14).

What was developed later on as Christian 'doctrine' can only be understood as the further development of this pointer to the basic fact. This is something essentially different from the proclamation of a systematic doctrine designed to give a comprehensive picture of God, man and the world, meant to be true for ever. Such a philosophy as that claims to be intelligible as a fabric of eternal truth quite independent of the one who teaches it. The Buddha explained to his disciples that, after his passing, his teaching would be their master. The significance of the Buddha as an individual was merely that he revealed to men a self-existent truth. If Christianity were nothing but a religious-ethical system of doctrines then its truths should also be able to stand independently of their proclaimer. But in Christianity it is quite a different matter. What it has to bring to bear is not a self-existent truth, or one that has perhaps vanished from the mind of man or never even entered it. Rather, what is pointed to is something entirely new to the world up to that time, something which, as a real factor of life, did not exist before.

But why should a doctrine drawing attention to the fact be added to the fact itself? Does not the fact alone suffice? The first Christians experienced it as deeply as possible; the nature of their inner attitude allowed them so strong a contact with it and to be so moved by the sheer volume of its power that they became 'in Christ' a 'new creation' (2Cor.5:17). But these forces of salvation proceeding from the deed of redemption do not take hold of one automatically. They are not obtrusive; one must open oneself to them. In order to do this, however, one needs to gain an awareness of how they can come in. The deed of redemption has been so arranged by Providence, one could say, that human freedom is not stifled. By means of a consciousness directed towards that fact, however, one can become prepared to open the door and let it enter into one's own being.

Thus the 'teaching' of Christianity concerns the fact, trying to bring home what *happened*, both to enable the mind to grasp it and the individual to make it his own. While the deed of the great Mystery is being enacted, the disciples prove unable to follow it with full consciousness. We see the significance of what Christ said to Peter at the Washing of the Feet: 'What I am doing you do not know now, but afterward you will understand' (John 13:7). This understanding afterwards is a matter of growth. The Holy Spirit—in the farewell discourses of John called the Paraclete, the Comforter who comforts by widening human consciousness—will lead into all truth (John 16:13), will teach all things, will bring to remembrance the words of Christ (John 14:26), will 'glorify' Christ, that is to say, reveal him more and more clearly to men (John 16:14). In the future he will even teach what the disciples 'cannot bear' now (John 16:12). Thus no limits are set to widening man's awareness of the fact of his redemption. The New Testament has nowhere, to quote Novalis, declared itself 'closed'. Occasionally the final verses of the Apocalypse have been used to support the argument that the revelation is closed, as they give a warning neither to add nor take away anything (Rev.22:18,19). But strictly speaking this relates to the words 'of this book', that is, the Apocalypse, whose words, since they arise from Inspiration, are meant to be protected by such a formal declaration. On principle, it can be said that the Christian's awareness of the fact of redemption and of the Being of Christ is always open to expansion.

Such an opportunity of gaining a knowledge of the supersensible as Anthroposophy can offer should not therefore be rejected by theologians just because its content goes beyond that of the New Testament. Whether or not what Anthroposophy has to say in this regard helps to extend the understanding of Christianity is a question to be answered by detailed examination. But a concept of the world which includes the supersensible should not be rejected *a priori*, for an understanding of the New Testament from a non-spiritual point of view is impossible. The New Testament, as already mentioned, does not contain a complete philosophical system as such. It takes for granted, however, a definite world concept which was widespread at that time. For example, Paul at one time speaks about a 'third heaven' (2Cor.12:2). This presupposes that there is a 'first' and 'second' heaven. Yet there is no other word about it in the New Testament. There was no need to present certain generally known ideas in a special systematic form to readers of that time. St. Paul occasionally mentions names for certain ranks in the angelic hierarchy, without any special piece of teaching being given on this in the New Testament. People knew what was meant. This picture of the world—taken as a matter of course in the New Testament—with the heavens, angels, demons and the realm of the dead, has been discredited in an age dominated by materialism. It is ridiculed as an obsolete, 'three-tiered' world outlook, and endeavours are made to demythologize the New Testament. If, however, one subscribes to a materialistic outlook, then the contents of the New Testament simply vanish. Anthroposophy, which has thoroughly assimilated the true achievement of scientific thinking and, still further, invaded new realms which could be called 'the lost provinces of human consciousness', is in a position to do justice to the outlook revealed by the Bible. The 'mythological' imagery makes sense if one recognizes the functioning of other forms of consciousness unknown to the mere intellect. In order to understand the Bible, theologians have collected an endless amount of working material for specialized study. To such specialized study, however, also belongs a knowledge of what Anthroposophy precisely describes as higher forms of human consciousness.

So it is not necessary from the very beginning to exclude the thought that the idea of reincarnation (as it appears in Anthroposophy) could take its part in broadening the Christian world picture; its expansion, as we have seen, is, in principle, possible. This will be followed up in detail. First of all the *basic fact* of the Christ-Event should be envisaged.

Christ Becoming Man

Christ brought *Himself*. That is the new fact. This new impact in the history of mankind is not only one in a series of foundings of religions; it is of an even higher order. It can be compared only with the *story of creation itself* as a second act in the creation of man. The divine act of creation narrated in Genesis completed man in regard to his bodily nature, which surpassed all other creations, but not yet in regard to his inner life. A being created in the image of God and destined to be independent and responsible could not go forth from the Creator's hand 'complete' like a creation in the realm of nature. He needed a 'history' of his own not required by the natural world. Although man, who came into existence on the sixth day of creation, was found 'very good', he had not yet reached his goal. This becomes apparent in Genesis, since the first chapter describing the initial creation of man is followed by a second chapter in which, seemingly once more, a creation of man is reported, but this time in a different way (Gen.2:7), being fashioned from the dust and given breath. This is followed by the division into two sexes (Gen.2:22). Critical analysis has shown that the beginning of Genesis presents us with two different accounts of the creation. It has been imagined that the editor of the text did not notice the incompatibility of the two versions and the combination was put down to his poor intelligence. Earlier Christian thinkers followed a different course. Their opinion was that the first chapter deals with a different plane, and the second descends from a level concerned only with the spirit, soul and life forces to one concerned more with earthly substance. So it would seem that the two accounts have been wisely combined just as we find them. The objection that the two parts differ in style and nomenclature and apparently stem from different 'schools' says nothing against the compiler of our present text having done just the right thing in referring the second story to a later stage. It is significant that the phrase 'the heavens and the earth' appears reversed in the second account as 'the earth and the heavens' (Gen.2:4).

Thus man descends deeper into the earthly world, but thereby arises the possibility of temptation and *falling into sin*. The childlike question, Who let the serpent into Paradise? draws our attention to a mystery: man at his creation was evidently not yet completed, but needed to meet the adversary, the 'experience' that had yet to be added to his original innocence. Nevertheless, this led him into the deepest tragedy. The independent being granted him is infected by Lucifer with egotism, and at the same time he entangles himself deeper in matter. The awareness of 'being naked' indicates that the one no longer sees the other in spirit but perceives only the physical body. The expulsion from the paradise of original oneness with God finally has *death* as its consequence. Falling a prey to death is not only 'punishment' but also grace in so far as it prevents mankind from perpetuating his fallen status (Gen.3:22). Death, that brought about for man in his separation from God the radical break in his existence on earth, is, as Paul puts it, 'the wages of sin' (Rom.6:23).

The first phase in the development towards the 'ego' leads into the isolation of self-centred egotism. The redeeming change into a 'selfless ego', which, just because it is in possession of itself can freely give of itself with love, is not within the power of man marked by the Fall. It is Christ who brings to mankind the power of the 'selfless ego'. This conferring of a power of love that had not before been active on earth opens *a second act in the creation of man* which, as already said, is not to be compared with any foundation of religion but only with the creation of the world itself. This, indeed, is what happens in the prologue of John's Gospel which opens with the very 'beginning', and then finds for the decisive deed of Christ the expression: 'And the Word became flesh' (John 1:14). From the Word 'in the beginning' to the Word that 'became flesh' the prologue of John covers an immense span of time.

If Christ wanted to bring the power of love to dwell in the selfless ego, He Himself had to incarnate. Along a way of voluntary sacrifice He had to follow man and meet him at the point he had reached. This way of sacrifice took the form of a *descent*. With true sovereignty, as one who 'descends' by his own wish, Christ pursued the way downwards which man, overpoweringly attracted from below, had himself gone as one who 'fell'. John's Gospel speaks forcefully again and again about this descent (*katabainein*) of Christ.

By descending, Christ reaches fallen mankind's sphere of existence which is called in the Bible 'flesh'. It is something momentous, which John's prologue expresses with uncompromising words: 'And the Word (*Logos*) became flesh (*sarx*)'. One could say, reversing a saying from Genesis (Gen.3:22): 'Behold, God has become like one of us.' The fact that Christ really had entered the frail human body, subject to death, is made abundantly clear in the Gospels. As a human being of flesh and blood, Christ is subject to fatigue (John 4:6) and the need for sleep (Matt.8:24); He feels hunger (Matt.4:2; 21:18) and thirst (John 4:7; 19:28); He weeps (Luke 19:41; John 11:35), He is 'very sorrowful, even to death' (Matt.26:38); in the 'agony' of His body, which at Gethsemane threatens almost to die prematurely, He sheds sweat like drops of blood (Luke 22:44).

The final consequence of the descent into *sarx* is *death*, the specific experience of men on earth. Only in death are the depths of earth experience finally reached. Anticipating this, Christ speaks about 'a baptism to be baptized with' (Luke 12:50). It is the price He has to pay in order to 'cast . . . upon the earth' the fire brought down from heaven. In the beginning of the synoptic Gospels a threefold baptism is described. John the Baptist baptizes 'with water', the 'mightier' One 'who is coming after' will baptize 'with the Holy Spirit and with fire' (Matt.3:11). Since the word *pneuma* in Greek means 'spirit' as well as 'air', these three baptisms show a relation to what for the ancient world were the 'elements'. Today, one would speak of 'physical states'. Passing through the four elements—earth, water, air and fire—which played a part in the Mysteries, was not only something external. The observable difference in quality between the solid, the liquid, the airy and the fiery in the material world was felt also as an expression of various kinds of inner experience. The step from 'earth' to 'water' was, as an inner experience, the transition from what was felt to be inflexible and rigid to something living, floating, streaming. In the airy element arose a feeling of being freed from the force of gravity, in fire of the light and warmth of divinity. The baptism of John was to bring mankind, fettered to the earth and, as it were, 'sitting on dry ground', a new connection with a purer, higher stream of life, to prepare an openness for the greater One who was to come. Then this greater One would lead earthly men into those still loftier and 'heavenly' ways of existence that could be divined in the flowing air (*pneuma*) and in fire. Since he is in need of redemption, it is primarily his earthly nature that man experiences on earth. The baptism with water, air and fire is to initiate him into higher realms. The conversation with Nicodemus (John 3:5) tells of the baptism with water and *pneuma*.

Descending into *sarx*, Christ brings with Him in His own heavenly being 'fire' and '*pneuma*' wherewith to baptize men. He Himself is not in need of such a baptism since being baptized means an immersion or initiation into an element of existence which one has previously stood outside. For the One descending from above it is necessary to be immersed in the lower elements that are the mark of earthly existence—water and earth, of which water still shows a certain kinship with heaven, being not yet so earthly as the element that gives its name to the whole planet 'the earth'. The descent of Christ is a way down to earth, indeed even to 'the heart of the earth' (Matt.12:40). The Baptism in Jordan is a *baptism with water*. Christ becomes connected with the ever moving life-element of the earth. But His full entry into the real 'earthly' is still to come, though in principle He has already taken hold of the earthly body. In the first period of His working in Palestine He prefers Galilee, the country round the lake. Capernaum, situated on the lake, is even called 'his own city' (Matt.9:1). There the great catch of fish occurs (Luke 5:1–11), the stilling of the storm, the meal near the lake and the walking on the water. When Christ, already set forth on His last journey to Jerusalem (Luke 9:51), speaks about His forthcoming 'baptism' He no longer means the Baptism in Jordan, but the final initiation into the element 'earth' that is still to come. But this is the experience of death in an earthly body. Facing this 'baptism' He says, 'and how I am constrained until it is accomplished!' (Luke 12:50)—literally, 'I am held together, pressed together'. It is the experience of oppressive restriction, whence comes the anguish. There is no word here of anxiety or dread in the normal sense, but of the terrible 'being pressed together' felt by a Spirit-Being, otherwise living in spacious realms of light, in the confinement of the earthly body bound for death.

The picture of the Death on Golgotha corresponds to this in its difference from the Baptism in Jordan. Over the Baptism in the Jordan heaven stands open: the voice of God sounds from above. Jesus stands in the flowing waters of the Jordan. Ancient church pictures have even presented Him clothed as in a watery bell. How different is Golgotha! There we are in stony Judaea. The rocky place is called 'the place of the skull'. On the hard wooden cross hangs the naked earthly body. Heaven is darkened. But the voice of God—'Thou art my beloved Son' —which rang out over the Baptism in Jordan now receives an echo from the earth. A representative of the Roman civilization so strongly attached to the earth, the Roman centurion, exclaims: 'Truly this was the Son of God!' (Matt.27:54). He makes the exclamation as a result of the impression made by the earthquake that came in response to this death. 'And the earth shook' (Matt.27:51). And while at the Baptism in Jordan the heavens opened—literally Mark says 'were torn open' (Mark 1:10)—now the earth opens: 'and the rocks were split; the tombs also were opened'.

This descent of Christ into *sarx*, completed on Golgotha, bears the stamp of 'once only'. Golgotha is an event that happened once and for all, as the Letter to the Hebrews emphatically indicates.

Research in the history of religions has become attentive to ancient myths and cults in which a dying 'redeemer-god' played a part. The uniqueness of Golgotha is not thereby called in question because those redeemer figures concerned remain in a sphere of uncertain ethereal images. They have never really walked the earth as Christ did who was crucified '*sub Pontio Pilato*' in harsh earthly reality. That event was *historical* and at the same time *mystically transparent*, as if making visible profound mysteries of the being of man. The cross as such, the three crosses, Jesus in the middle, the 'place of the skull', the crown of thorns, the darkening of the sun—all that is at the same time like a language of signs and runes. This part of earth history has the transparency of a mystery drama, the performance of a ritual. Lessing felt disturbed at Christianity being founded upon 'accidental historical events'. He was not aware of his assumption, made in a short-sighted and unsubstantiated manner, that all history must have the character of being 'accidental'. Among the events of history there is also something like an order of rank, a kind of hierarchy. Especially at important moments of history, the events themselves seem to tend to take on a pictorial significance. The Christ-Event in its uniqueness is history of the highest order, and is thus beyond all that is accidental. It occurred in a way that could not be different, both as history and as rite and rune. It is the *Word* that appears in the flesh.

The uniqueness of Golgotha excludes any application of the idea of reincarnation to the Christ's descent into *sarx*.

The Resurrection

As in dying the descending Christ has caught up with man on earth, so from Easter morning He goes before him, commanding the future as the supreme guide of life (*archegós*) (Acts 3:15). 'The Resurrection of Christ is the decisive fact of that whole higher history, though from the ordinary point of view incomprehensible. Facts such as Christ's Resurrection are like flashes of lightning by which the higher, that is the true inner history, breaks through into what merely shows outwardly. . . .' So Schelling said in the thirty-second lecture of his *Philosophy of Revelation*.

The Resurrection is more than the manifestation of one who has died proving to be still in existence. There has been experience of departed souls making themselves known elsewhere in humanity, too. The Resurrection concerns the *Body*.

What happened on Easter morning has something of a lightning suddenness. All four evangelists respect the mystery of that momentary glimpse by keeping silent; they refrain from saying anything about the occurrence itself. The fact of the Resurrection lives at first only in the consciousness of superhuman spiritual beings and comes to men first as a message from the angelic world. Already in the evening of Easter Sunday it finds its response in the consciousness of earthly men: 'The Lord has risen indeed' (*óntōs*—with his whole being) (Luke 24:34). And seven weeks later at Pentecost, awareness of it has gone so far that Peter not only proclaims the fact to his listeners, but opens for them a way of *inner access* to the event, though it nevertheless far surpasses all understanding. There is no dichotomy between its inscrutableness and eventual 'understanding' in connection with the Easter Fact. For human consciousness there is an approach that at least opens the way whereby one can divine that, far off as it may be, there will be a day when the mystery is comprehended. This first Christian message concerning such an unheard-of fact does not give the impression of simply being announced by Peter by virtue of apostolic authority and of his demanding its acceptance on authority. To the message: 'God raised him up, having loosed the pangs of death', he adds the clause: 'because it was not possible for him to be held by it' (Acts 2:24). 'Because it was not possible. . .' One does not speak thus about an event that hopelessly transcends all human understanding. One can only say such a thing if one has at least the beginnings of 'insight'. The reason for this Peter gives in what follows, which begins with the word 'for'. 'For David says concerning him . . .' And he quotes a passage from Psalm 16*. This psalm allows a glimpse back into the soul of a devout man of the Old Testament who, through the strength of his inner life, attains awareness of extraordinary vistas of hope. He begins by saying that he has 'the LORD always before me'. From such a life of permanent awareness of God's presence, profound bliss grows in his heart, radiating even into his body in which the God-devoted soul dwells—'moreover my flesh will dwell in hope'. And this hope opens a tremendous vista: 'For thou wilt not abandon my soul to Hades, nor let thy Holy One see corruption. Thou hast made known to me the ways of life' (Acts.2:25–28). Perhaps one might even see in Peter's quotation of the sixteenth Psalm a reminiscence of the teaching which according to Luke's Gospel the Risen One gave to His disciples about how they could find in the books of Moses, the Prophets and—expressly added—the Psalms 'what concerns me (*ta peri emou*)'. What the godly man experiences powerfully in his devout heart already here in earthly existence bears as it were a guarantee for the future, giving him hope for both soul and body after death. Thereby the devout man has set out on a way that finally leads to the Resurrection. What begins in the innermost spiritual centre of the heart bears in itself the power one day to take effect on soul and body. Where there exists only the first inkling of this, it may be said about Christ's Resurrection: 'because it was not possible' otherwise.

Peter bore in his soul yet another preparedness for the Easter Mystery that fell to his share by being present at the Transfiguration. Together with the other two chosen disciples he was privileged to witness how the countenance of Christ became as bright as the sun and the radiating light of glory spread even over His garments (Matt.17:2). This radiance of light spread from an inward event, from Christ's prayer (Luke

* See Rudolf Frieling, *Hidden Treasures in the Psalms*, Christian Community Press, London, 1967, p. 124ff.

9:28–29)*. Radiating from soul and spirit, the intense inner experience of the One who prays finally takes hold even of His body. *Metemorphóthe*—He was 'transfigured' say Matthew (17:2) and Mark (9:3). This is not yet the final and complete metamorphosis, but the Transfiguration definitely already lies on the path that eventually joins the Easter Mystery—itself specifically mentioned on the way down from the mountain of the Transfiguration. Christ commands the three disciples not to talk to anyone about this vision (*horama*) 'until the Son of man is raised from the dead' (Matt.17:9 and similarly Mark 9:9). The experience must not be fragmented by discussion. While silence is consciously maintained about it, it can work more powerfully in the soul. Finally, from such silent conservation and contemplation there comes forth as a ripe fruit on Easter Day a very first feeling of an understanding of the Resurrection. This in turn grows into the insight at Pentecost: 'because it was not possible' otherwise†.

The Resurrection, for all the lightning suddenness of its occurrence, is not a miracle beyond all understanding, but the climax of a discernible process that has preceded it. This can also be gathered from what Christ says at the grave of Lazarus to Martha, who had just hinted with a certain resignation at the raising of the dead hoped for on the Last Day. This saying of Christ falls into three parts. First: 'I am the resurrection and the life' (John 11:25). Thereby Christ says, 'The resurrection of which you have heard hitherto as a far off future goal—in me it is already present.' Already now, still during His earthly life, Christ inwardly senses the power of the Resurrection within Him. What He carries within Himself day by day during that earth existence as a permanent union with God gives Him the assurance of His power of resurrection. His awareness of the heavens does not relax even while He is bound to the *sarx*; it remains alert. He can say to His disciples, 'because I live, you will live also' (John 14:19), which certainly indicates: 'In you the

* See Rudolf Frieling, *Die Verklärung auf dem Berg*, Verlag Urachhaus, Stuttgart, 1969.

† It should also be noted that Luke, soon after the Transfiguration, records a saying of Christ that sounds as if it were spoken out of the experience of the Transfiguration, from a knowledge of a higher human body in preparation. 'If then your whole body is full of light, having no part dark, it will be wholly bright, as when a lamp with its rays gives you light (*photizein*)' (Luke 11:36).

higher consciousness is still only at a low level'. Considering those not yet spiritually awakened, He could speak of the 'dead' who should be allowed to bury their dead. Within Himself the Resurrection is already alive.

This leads to the second part of the statement: 'He who believes in me, though he die, yet shall he live'. He who opens himself to what exists in Christ's Being as resurrection and life is not yet, to be sure, removed from the fate of death. He must also die one day, but *then he dies differently*. He carries beyond death the higher life that has been aroused in him. This applies in the first place to Christ Himself. Dying, He knows 'today' He will be 'in Paradise' (Luke 23:43). After leaving the body, His soul will journey through the realm of the dead, bright as the sun and all-powerful in its ego-consciousness. To other departed souls, whose consciousness is diminished and who therefore take the other world as 'Hades', He can be the One who helps them to rise. It has been thought that the idea of being in Paradise contradicts the other idea of Hades, the shadow world of the dead, of the imprisoned spirits to whom, according to the First Letter of Peter (3:19; 4:6), Christ preached the Gospel after His death. Yet there is no reason for thinking there is a contradiction once Paradise and Hades are understood not as outer localities but as states of consciousness expressed in pictures. Just because Christ is in a 'Paradise' state after His death, He can radiate His own brightness of soul and spirit upon the departed souls who, without their bodies, find themselves in a 'Hades' state.

The Greek word '*Hades*' corresponds to the Hebrew '*Sheōl*', which also means the world of shadows, an underworld. Today's widespread criticism of the primitive 'three-tiered' world picture of antiquity is rather superficial. It is not sufficiently appreciated that for people of earlier times the supersensible and the material were very much more closely related. In its particular form and atmosphere, a landscape could be experienced as a 'landscape of the soul'—an inner mood. The sight of a gloomy, desolate landscape could open the inner eye for a corresponding condition of the soul, belonging to another level of existence. So the allegedly grossly superstitious idea that, say, a particular location should be regarded as an entrance to the realm of the dead would be understood and appreciated.

There is a real justification for a shadowy underworld. At birth the soul had descended to earth from realms of spiritual light, lived on earth in such a manner perhaps that, totally overwhelmed by earthly affairs, it more or less forgot its higher origin. In death, through abandoning the body, the soul is, as it were, 'repatriated' by force, but has lost the ability to perceive the spiritual world to any great extent. However bright the sunlight of the spiritual world may shine, he who has no eyes nevertheless walks in darkness. In other words: the ill-spent life on earth now brought to an end by death casts its shadow into the world beyond, thrusting itself between the spiritual sunlight and the departed soul. Hades is the Beyond overshadowed by the way of life completed on earth; it is, to use the words from the First Letter of Peter, the world of the 'spirits in prison'. It is a diminished existence in which they have the possibility neither of self-determination nor of perception of higher worlds and of working as spirit among spirits. The theory of 'Total Death' (*Ganztod*) will be considered later. First it suffices to say, in harmony with early Christian understanding, that the statement, 'though he die, yet shall he live' is, in its highest sense, applicable to Christ Himself. His Spirit-Soul was not wiped out by the death on the cross, but lived most vividly in the realm of the dead between Good Friday afternoon and Easter Sunday. As the Death on Golgotha —the last earthly consequence of Christ's descent into *sarx*— shook the earth (Matt.27:51), so again the earth is shaken on Easter morning (Matt.28:2). The events in the realm of the dead took place while the profound calm of the Sabbath was lying over Jerusalem (Luke 23:56). The earthquake of Easter morning indicates that something has happened that again concerns the earth.

We return to the words spoken at the grave of Lazarus: 'I am the resurrection and the life; he who believes in me, though he die, yet shall he live'. A third concluding sentence follows: 'and whoever lives and believes in me shall never die'. This even goes far beyond 'life in death'. Christ's statement culminates victoriously in the great and triumphant promise of 'never dying'. Not only does the bearer of higher life die differently— die in Christ like the first Christian martyr, Stephen (Acts 7:55–60)—not only shall death be experienced differently, but death itself shall be wholly eliminated. As man's fall into sin resulted in the death of the body, so the final result of the conquest of sin is the expulsion of death from the body. 'The last enemy to be destroyed is death' (1Cor.15:26). Then the earthly body which once forced Paul to cry in anguish, 'Who will deliver me from this body of death?' (Rom.7:24) will not only be permeated by the spirit as on the mount of the Transfiguration, but completely spiritualized.

The earthly body is the means whereby man gains consciousness of his own individuality. This self-awareness is tainted by egoism through the Fall, and this body death-stricken. Such as it is, it cannot yet be the instrument of his true ego. 'My' body is only to a certain extent 'mine' for it still carries the ancestral heritage. Only in a more or less limited way can a human body become the expression of the real individuality. Even Christ had to take on an hereditary body, but, dwelling therein as the great selfless Ego, He was able through the spirit to make it more and more His own. He could truly say at the Last Supper 'my' body, 'my' blood. Just for that reason He could have completely at His disposal what was truly His, and out of His selfless Ego give it completely away: 'Take this . . .' One can only give what is one's own. In Christ, 'ego' and 'mine' regain their true meaning, not as the expression of egotistical possession, but simply as the basis for selfless giving. This body, already so far permeated and spiritualized by Christ, now becomes at last 'His' body, the final and fitting instrument of His true Being, through the great mystery of the transformation on Easter morning.

The Resurrection Body is metamorphosed out of the earthly body. It would not have come into being without it. There is a continuity that shows itself in the marks of the wounds (John 20:20–27). In the account of Easter given by Luke it is particularly emphasized that it was not a question of the spirit of a dead man appearing (24:37) as the disciples at first imagined. There had always been appearances of that kind. But here it is a different matter. The Risen One shows His hands and feet, whereby the disciples may see 'that it is I myself (*ego eimi autos*)' (24:39)—the strongest expression of individual identity. This individual identity reveals and makes itself active in the form of the human body, whereby man alone, in contrast to the animals, can truly speak of 'hand' and 'foot'. Furthermore, 'flesh and bones' are mentioned, which a mere disembodied spirit 'has not'. Flesh—consequently *sarx*. There cannot be any question of solid matter since the Resurrection Body goes through closed doors (John 20:19), can become visible and again vanish (*aphantos*) 'out of their sight' (Luke 24:31). But the word '*sarx*', never used in the synoptic Gospels in regard to Christ except in this place, forcefully indicates the continuous connection with the body of Jesus that He bore towards death. The same with the word 'bones'. Man's skeleton is a miraculous structure, made visible, indeed, through material particles, but, as such, a divinely conceived form. The earthly matter has fallen off, the form created by the spirit temporarily becomes visible for the disciples to see. Moreover, what the disciples experience as the Risen One's 'eating' (Luke 24:42–3) also points to the existence of a body, and we leave it open whether it was a question of a vision or something like a dematerialization. Eating and drinking always meant for the disciples while living with their master very much more than just ordinary nourishing.

Here one should take into account that the Body, which is the guarantee of the connection and identity, really has undergone a metamorphosis beyond all conception. What Paul explains concerning the future resurrection body hoped for by men—that 'flesh and blood' unchanged 'cannot inherit the kingdom of God' (1Cor.15:50), that 'this perishable nature must put on the imperishable, and this mortal nature must put on immortality (*athanasia*)' (1Cor.15:53) whereby 'death is swallowed up in victory' (1Cor.15:54)—all this happens to Christ already on Easter morning. What is for man a far-distant goal —at the Last Day, at the end of this aeon—Christ has achieved for Himself 'already now' on Easter Day, in those three days striding powerfully, as if with god-like steps, through the span of time that still separates man from the Last Day. *The Resurrection on Easter Day, as it were, is nothing less than a part of the Last Day, inoculated from the coming aeon into our own age.* Here indeed 'the future has already begun'. This fact is unique and so tremendous that, as Schelling said, one must find courage 'in one's heart' if one wants to approach it, 'because it is the heart above all that is needed for the magnitude of the subject' (*Philosophy of Revelation*, Lecture 24).

The Ascension

Although the Resurrection seemed to come like a flash of lightning on Easter morning, it was in fact the culmination of a long silent evolution which encompassed the inner life of the incarnate Christ during His earthly life, the events of Maundy Thursday and Good Friday, and what happened in the realm of the dead on Holy Saturday. After the decisive Easter morning a further development can also be discerned in which what has been born out of death strengthens its existence still further. On Sunday morning it is still so sensitive that it cannot stand human contact. '*Noli me tangere*.' One week later at the meeting with doubting Thomas it is already different (John 20:17 and 20:27). 'Do not hold me' is explained: 'for I have not yet ascended to the Father.' Further on the saying is in the present tense: 'I am ascending to my Father. . . .' So He is already on that path which leads Him to the Father. Since He invites Thomas a week later to touch, to take hold of Him, it seems that in between He must have gone some way further on the path on which He set out on Easter morning. The Father bears within Himself the most profound and fundamental powers of the world—'He is greater than I' (John 14:28). While going towards the Father the Risen One imbues the newly born Resurrection Body more and more with those profound and fundamental powers, making its existence ever more real. John does not describe the event of the Ascension forty days after Easter, but with the saying of Easter morning—'I am ascending to my Father'—he indicates something in the nature of a process which is then completed on the actual day of the Ascension.

The Ascension as described by Luke suggests at first that Christ was going away from His followers. He is lifted up and disappears into the clouds. Here again, Christian theology need not fear objections about an obsolete three-tiered view of the world. The 'breaking open' of heaven at the Baptism was not an event observable by everybody. Only Jesus and John 'saw' it. Still, they did not imagine it; it was a true vision seen in a picture whose elements are taken from the physical world. The wide-reaching dome of the light-filled sky above us, primarily only a visual impression, provides the picture in which the spiritual vision is presented. Through it the fact is revealed that a spiritual being, hitherto at home in higher supersensible realms, now abandons that position and moves His existence to the earthly world. The One who descended (how right this term is!) has now completed His journey into the *sarx*, and from the *sarx* has wrested the metamorphosed spiritual Resurrection Body. This achievement, gained on earth, He now carries up in order to make it part of the higher realms. The Letter to the Hebrews describes how the One who passed through Golgotha bears His deed of sacrifice into the Holy of Holies in heaven. So far the inhabitants of higher worlds have lived outside the experience of death, which can be experienced only on earth in a human body. Hölderlin, in harmony with the ancient Greeks, could look up to those dwelling in heaven: 'You live above in the light . . .' feeling all the more painfully, 'but we . . .' This has changed through Christ's becoming man. Coming from beyond the sphere of our human sin-burdened fate, He joined forces with mankind in voluntary sacrifice by accepting the experience of death in His divine soul, 'tasting' death (Heb.2:9). Since then, there is in heaven the *God with the marks of the wounds* (Rev.5:6). Something that did not exist before in the heavenly realms has now been added from the earth. The Deed of Golgotha could be accomplished only on the earth. The First Letter of Peter even says that 'angels long to look' in order to perceive what has been done by Christ (1Pet. 1:12). Filling the old words of Isaiah (65:17) with new Christian content, John's Apocalypse speaks not only of a 'new earth' to come, but also of a 'new heaven' (Rev.21:1, also 2Pet.3:13). The angelic realms above are enriched by what radiates upwards from the earth; they are refreshed and rejuvenated by what Christ bears up to them. The fact that the Resurrection Body, born out of death on earth, becomes part of the higher realms is the background to the picture of the Ascension.

It is remarkable how strongly the 'seeing' of the disciples plays a part in Luke's account. He was lifted up 'as they were looking on' (Acts 1:9). The cloud took Him out of their 'sight'. 'While they were gazing into heaven . . .'(1:10). 'Why do you stand looking into heaven?' (1:11). He 'will come in the same way as you saw him go into heaven' (1:11). It is not a question of a miraculous levitation of a material body, nor something that everyone could have seen. It is a clairvoyant experience of the disciples. The vanishing into the clouds is the pictorial expression of the experience that the Resurrection Body, previously occasionally within reach of their visionary power, now moves beyond the range of that power; they can no longer keep up with its further spiritualization, and experience this as His 'vanishing'.

After the descending, the *katabainein* so emphatically stated in John's Gospel, there follows from Easter onwards the ascending, the *anabainein*. Christianity need not be ashamed of the words 'descending' and 'ascending' as if they belonged to an outdated mode of thinking. Moving up and down are absolutely correct terms if taken as a movement of consciousness between different levels of existence. They are part of the fundamentally precise picture language of the Bible. Jacob, the patriarch, beholds in a dream the *heavenly ladder* which connects the Above with the Below. 'There was a ladder set up on the earth, and the top of it reached to heaven; and behold, the angels of God were ascending and descending on it' (Gen.28:12). At the beginning of creation, heavenly Above and earthly Below were separated from each other in order through their polarity to provide a field of tension as a stage for mankind. The two worlds should fructify each other. There is a constant stream of forces from above downwards, another from below upwards. Those dwelling in higher worlds, angelic beings, are moving in both directions. They continually carry the heavenly to earth, and from mankind on earth they have to bear upward and unite with heaven what can be created only on earth.

At one point in John's Gospel an angel is mentioned who descends into the Pool of Beth-zatha (5:4) while the water is moving and brings the healing forces to it. Angels do not descend so far that they incorporate, yet perhaps this angel at Beth-zatha was able to form itself over the spray into a transitory body-like form which could be perceived by some still clairvoyant people. But man himself descends more completely to the earth. From it he is to gain his independence and then bear the result up to higher realms. But his descent into incarnation—as such, the will of God—became a 'fall'. He has succumbed to the pull from below and thereby the harmonious intercommunication between heaven and earth is disturbed. The angels find less and less of what is worth carrying up; man's earthly existence closes itself more and more against what the angels wish to bring down. When a man dies he finds it difficult to relate himself to the upward movement. By becoming Man, Christ restores the original relation between Above and Below. In connection with the ancient vision of Jacob, He speaks of heaven that will again stand open over the earth, and of 'angels of God ascending and descending upon the Son of man' (John 1:51). He Himself executes on a grand and unique scale this ascending and descending intended for man. His descending leads to the death on Golgotha and to Hades, while in His Easter-Ascension movement upwards He carries with Him the Resurrection Body wrested free from the earth.

His vanishing from the disciples' sight should not be taken as contradicting what the Risen One said: 'Lo, I am with you always'. The Ascension is even the prerequisite for the fulfilment of this promise. During His life as Jesus, the Christ existed only for those who crossed His path because they were living in Palestine at that time. Some Greeks ask for Him one day and Christ takes this as a sign that 'the hour has come for the Son of man to be glorified (*doxazein*)' (John 12:23)—the glorification, the great metamorphosis through which He reaches such a mode of existence that He can exist for all men. By becoming permeated with the 'heavenly', the Resurrection Body is freed from all limitations. It is then embodied in the spiritual world as a centre of forces lifted beyond space, yet able to work from this spiritual world 'everywhere' into space. We shall come back to this later.

After also considering the uniqueness and finality of the 'ascending' through the Resurrection and Ascension, we should make it quite clear once more, as we did after the consideration of Christ's descent (p. 22), that in the framework of *these* events there is absolutely no room for reincarnation, since Christ, with mighty, God-like strides through Easter and Ascension, has Himself already reached the Last Day, which for man is still a far-distant goal.

Yet it might be asked whether, perhaps, Christ's 'coming again', the *Parousia*, has something to do with reincarnation. The story of the Ascension gives a key to that. As Christ vanishes from their sight, the disciples hear the angels say that He 'will come in the same way as you saw him go into heaven' (Acts 1:11). In the same way as He disappeared into the clouds He will again in the future appear out of the clouds* before men's eyes (Matt.24:30;26:64;1Thess.4:17;Rev.1:7;14:14). The realm of the clouds, where continual forming and re-forming goes on, is at the same time like a picture of the sphere of 'possibilities' surrounding our earth. It is the part of the earth where everything is still flexible, where anything can come about, but which also receives the radiations and influences of the surrounding heavens. In this sphere where earth and heaven meet, in this realm of future possibilities, Christ holds sway since the day of the Ascension. Out of this form of existence He can be present for all men without restriction. 'I am with you always.' At first this new form of existence went beyond the visionary power of the disciples. The promise of His coming again is just as little a contradiction of the saying, 'I am with you' as the Ascension is. The 'coming' is a 'coming to awareness' of His already established presence. That 'He is with us' does not necessarily mean that 'we are with Him'—just as a nurse watching the sleep of a sick man is certainly with him, but the sleeping man is not with the nurse as long as he is not awake and aware of the fact. The presence of Christ since the Ascension is at first hidden from men. The promise of His coming points towards a future awakening of mankind to this mysterious presence. 'As you saw him go into heaven—in the same way he will come.' In the future the visionary power will awaken and continue just where it once broke off for the disciples. The 'coming' brings a 'broadening of consciousness' for men, who will then have a direct experience of the reality of Christ's presence, just as Paul himself did at Damascus. The fact that the coming will occur in the realm of the clouds clearly indicates that it is not a question of Christ's coming back into earthly *sarx*. That would be absolutely nonsensical in view of the fact that the Resurrection Body has achieved the final perfection. The fact that Christ does not reincarnate in an earthly body was the decisive point of difference when, in 1912–13, the separation came between Rudolf Steiner and the Theosophical Society,

* For the cloud motif see Friedrich Benesch: *Das Ereignis der Himmelfahrt Christi*, Verlag Urachhaus, Stuttgart, 1974.

within whose framework he had worked at first, though independently. It is worth noticing that the founder of the modern anthroposophical teaching of reincarnation emphasized both that a return of Christ in the flesh as expected in those days in theosophical circles is out of the question, and that with such an idea the true knowledge of the being and uniqueness of Christ would be completely missed.

The same understanding applies to the 'coming again'; *To Christ Himself the idea of reincarnation is not applicable.*

Christ Himself and His work are the factual basis of Christianity. But now this work, itself a reality, requires to be understood, affirmed and inwardly grasped in freedom by mankind. The whole idea of 'Christianity' also includes the understanding that, as a response to Christ becoming man, man should become Christian. We turn now to this other aspect of Christianity and then again pursue the question of reincarnation.

Man Becoming Christian

In the Letter to the Philippians Paul writes: 'Not that I have already obtained this or am already perfect; but I press on to make it my own, because Christ Jesus has made me his own' (3:12). In the First Letter of John we read: 'It does not yet appear what we shall be' (3:2). In the Sermon on the Mount there occurs the extraordinary saying: 'You, therefore, must be perfect, as your heavenly Father is perfect' (Matt.5:48).

There should be no doubt about it that becoming Christian really means what it says: it is 'a becoming', a matter of *growing*, something involving development. The New Testament is full of hints of the inner working through which all that is imperfect in man 'so far' (really there as 'raw material') could be changed by virtue of his union with Christ. Paul, so strongly warning against the complacency of the Pharisees, who suppose they can appear before God through 'good deeds', still makes the following demand: 'Have this mind among yourselves, which you have in Christ Jesus' (Phil.2:5). In John's Gospel the question about doing good deeds is answered with the words: 'This is the work of God, that you believe in him whom he has sent' (John 6:29). Here, then, 'believing' means opening oneself to Christ so that His Being can enter in. As a result, without particular effort, the good deeds come about of higher necessity. But come about they must, otherwise belief would not be what it should. Belief by no means excludes the element of self-discipline. Paul admonishes Timothy: 'Train yourself in godliness' (1Tim.4:7. Greek *gymnazein*). The Letter to the Hebrews speaks of faculties of perception (*aisthetēria*) of a higher order to be 'trained by practice' (5:14). Without activity on the part of the believer, what Paul describes in the Second Letter to the Corinthians (3:18) as the reflecting of Christ's likeness (*eikōn*) in our unveiled faces cannot come about. Without our active will there is no possibility for what he describes as exposing ourselves to the radiance of the original image, whereby the change can take place 'from one degree of glory to another'. Even the word 'progress' (*prokopé*) is used by Paul concerning inner Christian development—in the Letter to the Philippians (1:25) and to Timothy (1Tim.4:15); likewise the concept of 'degree' (*bathmos*), rendered in Latin as *gradus* (1Tim.3:13).

The experience of grace does not exclude individual effort, which can even open the way for the awareness of grace. The interweaving of personal striving and grace has been expressed in the classic paradox by Paul in the Letter to the Philippians: 'Work out (*katergázesthe*) your own salvation with fear and trembling; *for God is at work* in you, both to will and to work (*energein*) for his good pleasure' (2:12–13). The same in John's Gospel: 'Do not *labour* for the food which perishes, but for the food which endures to eternal life, which the Son of man will *give* to you' (6:27). Labour for what will be given!

That the development of a Christian is not a matter of striving after a pattern, which as such remains outside him, is shown clearly in the Pauline and Johannine expression of the 'indwelling'. 'I have been crucified with Christ; it is no longer I who live, but Christ who lives in me' (Gal.2:20). 'You in me, and I in you' (John 14:20). The ego, wherein the individual is conscious of himself, is the highest element in man. If Christ is accepted therein, the process of metamorphosis gradually permeates the whole human being and finally reaches the depths of his body. 'Therefore, if any one is in Christ, he is a new creation (*ktisis*)' (2Cor.5:17). In becoming Christian, it is a matter of the whole human being experiencing a union, accepting an absolutely real influence into his own being; this is experienced in the Eucharist which has been celebrated in Christendom from the beginning (Acts 2:46). In John's account of the Feeding of the Five Thousand, which seems like an anticipation of the mystery of the Eucharist just a year before Golgotha, the relationship of the Christian to Christ is expressed in the shortest way: 'He who eats me . . .' (6:57). The unifying process begins in the spiritual region of the soul, yet the further it goes the deeper it invades the lower levels of the human being, till it finally reaches the body. The early Christians felt vitally that through the bread and wine of the Eucharist they were connected with the Resurrection Body of Christ; the Communion was for them *pharmakon athanasias*, medicine for immortality.* The experience of Communion gave them a foretaste of future perfection. *Athanasia*—Paul uses this word when he speaks of the future resurrection body, the mortal putting on 'immortality (*athanasia*)' (1Cor.15:53). Thus a connection between the Eucharist and the Last Day becomes evident.

In the sixth chapter of John's Gospel the experience of Communion and the Last Day are significantly brought together. In connection with the Feeding of the Five Thousand, Christ speaks first of the 'bread of life' (three times: 6:35,48,51). The third time He goes on to be still more specific: 'And the bread which I shall give for the life of the world is my flesh' (6:51). In the New Testament, *kosmos* (world) does not mean what we call the cosmos today, but the world of man in need of redemption. It is remarkable that instead of 'body' (*soma* as at the institution of the Eucharist) Christ uses the word '*sarx*,' flesh—which concerned us earlier. Is not this expression too coarse, especially in the most spiritual of the four Gospels? One feels the disciples were not altogether wrong when they took offence at the 'hard' (*sklerós*) saying (6:60). We should remember that we do not meet this word here for the first time in John's

* Letter of Ignatius to the Ephesians 20:2.

Gospel. It occurs with greatest significance in the prologue: 'The Word became flesh'. In the prologue the evangelist lets there be no doubt that Christ really did descend into the human earthly body, that He did not remain in a more ethereal form above the level where man meets death. Through the use of just that word in connection with the experience of Communion it is made clear, in a drastically radical way, that the body to be received in Communion would not exist without Christ's entry into the sphere of *sarx*. It is a similar radicalism of expression as in Luke's chapter on the Resurrection where 'flesh and bones' of the Risen One are mentioned. The Body that is effectual in the Eucharist could be metamorphosed only out of an earthly, mortal body. In the course of Christ's later teaching it becomes evident that the word *sarx* is obviously the preliminary to transubstantiation, without which mere *sarx* would be 'of no avail' (6:63). But Christ's body of flesh has been permeated and spiritualized by the life-giving spirit and is therefore not only not 'of no avail', but just by virtue of this metamorphosis something of supreme and ultimate value.

Whenever Christ speaks of His 'flesh' and 'blood' as gifts needed for the salvation of the communicant, nothing 'merely pictorial' is meant, but a true spiritual reality. The Jews took offence at the 'hard' saying: 'Who can listen to it?' (John 6:60). 'How can this man give us his flesh to eat?' (6:52). Even among Christ's followers uncertainty arises (6:61). What does Christ answer? He hints at His coming Ascension. 'Do you take offence at this? Then what if you were to see the Son of man ascending where he was before?' (6:61–62). How far is this reference to the Ascension a help towards understanding? It was surely given for those in doubt.

When the Reformers argued with Luther about the Eucharist they asserted that, through the Ascension, the body of the Lord was taken away from the earth and therefore could not be on the altars of Christian churches as a 'real presence', bread and wine being mere symbols. The bread 'is' not Christ's Body but only 'signifies' it. With this argument, the Reformers show themselves no longer able to take the Ascension in an imaginative way, debasing it to an outer, localized event and thereby missing the real level of existence to which it belongs. The logic, of course, is striking: a body that is in heaven cannot be on earth, and at the same time on many altars. A higher Christian wisdom or Christian esotericism was foreign to Luther; he did not have at his disposal a world-concept embracing supersensible facts. It is all the more remarkable that from a deep religious instinct he does not succumb to the shortcomings of Zwingli's logic and, with a sure feeling that something is here at stake that must never be lost to Christianity, maintains the truth of the 'real presence' in the Eucharist. Not: 'it signifies' but 'it is . . .'. In this connection, his writings, *The Words Still Remain* (1527) and *Great Confession to the Lord's Supper* (1528), and his teaching on 'ubiquity' evolve thoughts which bring him far closer to the mystery of the Eucharist than Zwingli. A right understanding of the Ascension is also at stake for it is of key importance in this matter. Luther knows that the Ascension is misunderstood if one considers only the material mode of existence, the 'comprehensible bodily mode in which He [Christ] physically walked on earth, taking up and leaving space according to His actual size (*quantitas*) . . . He does not exist in such a way . . . in heaven . . . ; since God has no spatial body . . .. Furthermore [there is] the incomprehensible spiritual mode of existence in which He neither takes nor leaves space, but permeates all creatures according to His will . . .. Thirdly [there is] the divine heavenly mode, since He is one person with God, whereby all creatures are of course bound to be very much more open and accessible to Him.' He who ascends to heaven sits at God's right hand, but 'God's right hand is everywhere'. 'He has not climbed up to heaven on a ladder or come down on a rope.' Luther speaks of the 'way His [Christ's] divine Being can exist wholly and completely in all creatures, and in each in a special way, even more profoundly, intimately and actually than the creature to himself . . .'.

The Ascension does not exclude the presence of Christ's Body and Blood at the Eucharist but on the contrary makes it actually possible by carrying over the Resurrection Body of Christ into an unrestricted form of existence which can be everywhere—(what Luther called 'ubiquity'). Thus, Communion is not a mere symbol, but provides, to quote Luther once more: 'a powerful food . . . the food is so powerful that it changes us completely, and out of carnal, sinful, mortal men makes spiritual, holy, immortal men, which we also are already, though it is hidden in faith and in hope and not yet apparent: at the Last Day only, we shall see it'.

We return to the sixth chapter of St. John's Gospel. Having introduced the offending word '*sarx*' in what He said on the Bread of Life, Christ speaks not less than four times about 'flesh and blood'. At first the flesh and blood 'of the Son of man' (6:53), then in 6:54,55,56 each time 'my' flesh, 'my' blood. In 6:54 His words on Communion make a link with others that went before. First He says (6:39): 'I should lose nothing of all that he [the Father] has given me, but raise it up (*anastēso*) at the last day'. Once more in a slightly changed way (6:40): 'For this is the will of my Father, that every one who sees the Son and believes in him should have eternal life; and I will raise him up at the last day'. For the third time (6:44): 'No one can come to me unless the Father who sent me draws him; and I will raise him up at the last day'. Finally, in the fourth and last instance, the connection is made between this idea of the 'last day' and Communion: 'He who eats my flesh and drinks my blood has eternal life, and I will raise him up at the last day' (6:54). It should not be overlooked that a statement parallel in construction (6:40) precedes this sentence by way of preparation. To clarify the metamorphosis that takes place from one to the other, we will set both down:

6:40: For this is the will of my Father,
that everyone who sees the Son
and believes in him
should have eternal life;
and I will raise him up
at the last day.
6:54: He who eats my flesh
and drinks my blood
has eternal life,
and I will raise him up
at the last day.

The sentences are alike in construction. What is twofold in 6:40: 'who sees the Son' 'and believes in him' is metamorphosed in 6:54 into the twofold 'eats' and 'drinks'. The first version—*sees and believes*—at a first glance seems 'more spiritual' than the second—*eats and drinks*. But one should note the value given them by their position. The second version in comparison with the first goes further. Were the sequence reversed—first *eat and drink* and then *see and believe*—one could take as a mere pictorial expression and misinterpret what is meant to be a spiritual reality. But it begins with what concerns soul and spirit: *see and believe*. Man's relation to Christ commences with becoming aware of him, knowing him by sight (in Greek, *theorein*). Thereby the 'contours' of his 'form' are comprehended. What follows as 'believing' means the growing participation in the power pulsating through that form; it is an experience of great strength. The metamorphosis described in verse 54 lies in this: because he has looked with devotion, man will receive into himself the true form of Christ. The form to whose radiance he 'exposes' himself begins to impress itself into him. This process culminates in the acceptance of Christ's body. —'Who eats my flesh'—what began in soul and spirit gradually comes to include the whole human being right down to the physical body. 'Seeing' becomes Communion with the Body. The Resurrection Body is not material, but pure form. 'Believing', which has a dynamic quality about it, grows gradually towards receiving the divine strength that flows in the blood of Christ's body, so that 'believing in him' becomes 'drinking his blood'. Seeing and believing remain as a spiritual preliminary, but this goes on to reach ever deeper into the world of physical existence. In ancient Greek terms, seeing would be an Apollonian, believing a Dionysian experience. The Eucharist contains both. There are profound reasons for the twofold 'body' and 'blood'.

In such a Communion, eternal life is experienced 'already now'; yet its full effect will become evident at 'the last day'.

The Last Day, *escháte heméra*—in regard to the end of the world, the expression is absolutely right. It is the right expression in so far as space and time in our sense will one day cease to exist. Man has been placed in an earth existence, which itself does not last for ever, in order to become truly man. This arrangement of Providence for man's earth existence is only an episode (however long it may appear to us to have lasted), and when it ends it will be seen whether he has achieved this aim—becoming truly himself in absolute freedom, something he could achieve only under those particular conditions of existence. The result will be apparent in the resurrection body he then bears into eternity, by virtue of which he will be 'wholly himself' even in eternal realms of the spirit. What has not been achieved at the end of time can no longer be attained in any other way. The Last Day is also The Last Judgment.

The Gospel of St. John—in a similar way also the Apocalypse—shows to a remarkable degree the significance of the use of sacred numbers. Thus the phrase 'The Last Day' occurs exactly seven times, four of which are in the sixth chapter. At the Feast of Tabernacles it signifies the seventh and last day of the festival (7:37), but there also it has an eschatological-apocalyptic ring to it. The festival week becomes like a parable, its 'last day' giving a feeling of the future end of the world. It is called the 'great' day and on it Christ speaks of the 'rivers of living water' which will flow from the bodies of those who believe in Him—this also being a promise of changed bodily existence. At the grave of Lazarus (11:24), Martha speaks of the 'last day'. In her mouth it sounds like something learnt from the catechism. But her words provide Christ with the opportunity of announcing this far distant goal to be 'already now' revealed in Himself, right in the present aeon: 'I am the resurrection . . .' For the seventh and last time the 'last day' is mentioned at the end of Christ's outer activities on earth, when, before His Passion begins, those retrospective, epilogue-like words are spoken: 'He who rejects me and does not receive my sayings has a judge; the word that I have spoken will be his judge on the last day' (12:48).

Between Death and the Last Day

Through His Resurrection, whereby He realized the Last Day in advance in His own person, Christ became 'the first-born from the dead' (Col.1:18), 'the first fruits of those who have fallen asleep' (1Cor.15:20). He is 'the first-born among many brethren' (Rom.8:29) destined to be made into the likeness (*sym-morphos*) of His image (*eikón*). The word '*sym-morphos*' is also used by Paul in his Letter to the Philippians (3:21): the Christ who ascended 'will change our lowly body to be like (*sym-morphon*) his glorious body'.

This is the great and ultimate goal of the Last Day. Yet we have seen that it is already being prepared in the earthly life of Christians. The *permeation with Christ* begins when the striving Christian soul turns with all its inner strength towards the figure of Christ Jesus and His destiny on earth. Devoutly contemplating the events of Christ's Passion, it is finally led through sympathy, its ability to share sorrow, to a real suffering with Christ. Paul described the crucified Christ to the Galatians as if He had been crucified 'before' their 'eyes' (Gal.3:1). He himself so lived through the Passion that he could feel in his own body the marks of the wounds, the 'stigmata' (Gal.6:17). He can say about himself: 'I die every day' (1Cor.15:31), but in a different sense from his contemporary, Tiberias, who wrote in a letter to the senate: '*perire me cotidie sentio* (I feel myself perishing daily)' (Tacitus, Ann.VI.6). Paul's experience is one of 'dying and becoming': 'Though our outer nature is wasting away, our inner nature is being renewed every day' (2Cor.4:16).

Paul endeavours to lead his congregations to a true inner participation in what Christ originally experienced on earth. Thus what is at first sym-pathy becomes 'sym-passion'—suffering-with (Rom.8:17), being crucified-with (Rom.6:6; Gal.2:20), dying-with (2Cor.7:3), being buried-with (Rom.6:4; Col.2:12), being raised-with (Eph.2:6; Col.2:12), living-with (2Cor.7:3; 2Tim.2:11), being glorified-with (Rom.8:17). Through all this, Christ is to establish His own form in Christian souls (*morphothé* Gal.4:19). This metamorphosis through the permeation by the great Original is to come about gradually—'from one degree of glory to another' (2Cor.3:18).

This process of development in 'becoming Christian' moves towards the distant goal of the Last Day. For each individual, would-be Christian it begins in a different way. It is broken off by death which meets Christian souls at various stages of 'becoming Christian' according to age, destiny, maturity and degree of striving. *How is this process of development related to its fulfilment on the Last Day? What lies between death and the Last Day?*

The answer given by the recently developed theological doctrine of 'Total Death' (*Ganztod*) is that between a man's death and his resurrection on the Last Day there is absolutely nothing. Death as payment for sin concerns the whole man and casts him totally into nothingness. He exists only in the memory of God who will create him anew, as it were, on the Last Day. This doctrine of complete extinction through death is felt to be in accord with the modern naturalistic view of man as an inseparable unit of body and soul, and rejects the idea of the soul's existence apart from the body.

Never before, apart from Jehovah's Witnesses, was there such a teaching in Christianity. It is an age-old human experience that the soul is not merely a phenomenon that appears and disappears with the body, but it is an experience to which a one-sided intellectual outlook cannot do justice. The 'Total Death' theory, however, is even supported on religious grounds. It is felt to be presumptuous for man to claim immortality for his soul and try to get away from the death sentence his sin deserves. The First Letter to Timothy is referred to where it is said of God that He 'alone has immortality (*athanasia*)' (1Tim.6:16). But since God according to Christian thinking has His being in 'love' (1John 4:16), one is entitled to think that He would therefore let other beings participate in what is His—in the sense of His great offering at the Last Supper: 'Take . . .'. The doctrine of a totally transcendental God would be Muslim rather than Christian. If it is true that the spiritual essence of man is not destroyed through death, then it depends on the divinely created order of things; and if it appears as man's actual spiritual experience, he cannot be regarded as laying claim to his immortality as if it were a legal right. Paul also uses the word '*athanasia*', as we have seen, in regard to the future resurrection body which will come into being through the great change: 'For this perishable nature must put on the imperishable, and this mortal nature put on immortality' (1Cor.15:53). It would be mistaken to suppose that man would not be deeply affected by the threatened death penalty following his fall into sin if it concerned only his body, which in itself is innocent. The punishment that really hits home for a sinful man who, relying on his bodily nature, separates himself from the divine, rests on the fact that in death the body which has allowed him such emancipation is taken away from him as payment for the misuse of his independence. Annihilation for the soul would be no punishment. Contemplation of a misused incarnation is a much more serious judgment than non-existence, which is not painful. The arguments for the theory of 'Total Death' are not convincing. Nor are the references to the Bible which come repeatedly into conflict with what the Bible actually says, although it is true that in both the Old and New Testaments the emphasis is on the resurrection of the body.

In the chapter, 'Fact and Doctrine', we said that it is a matter of seeing that the whole condition of the world has begun to change fundamentally through Christianity. It is not in itself a system of existing truths about God and the world presented in the Bible like a compendium. This also holds good for the Old Testament. Here, too, it is not first and foremost a question of a body of timeless doctrines but of a series of events stretching over thousands of years and finally concentrating in the Israelites, who are overshadowed by the messianic promise of a great, world-wide salvation. Israel has the unique task of providing the earthly body for the coming redeemer. This determines the direction of the whole history of salvation in the Old Testament. With Christ's coming, the history of Israel ceases to be the history of salvation; it culminated in the Incarnation, the redeemer becoming flesh.

The Old Testament, therefore, concerns itself chiefly with the earth and man on earth. His propagation there is an important matter from a religious point of view; the Messiah's body is prepared through the ancestral line of Abraham and David. The Incarnation, in accordance with the divine order, also has its own particular place on earth, the promised land, *erets Israel.* Concentration on the earthly body involves even the eschatological-apocalyptic writers in looking towards the *ultimate* resurrection of the body and so disregarding the spiritual state of man immediately after death. The great visions of the prophets, so full of hope, concern the *body* (Isa. 25:8; 26:19; Ezek.37; Dan.12:2; Hos.6:2; Job 19:26; Ps.16:9; 49:15; 73:24), though from the admittedly few passages in the Psalms one could just as soon think of conditions after death *before* the final resurrection.

There is no need to point out an absolute contradiction between the Old Testament (and even the New) and Platonism. The Greeks had a different task from that of Israel. With Plato particularly, the ancient transcendental wisdom from the Mysteries came to light once more. Those who were spiritually inclined could experience their supersensible existence. Plato felt that the bodily condition can offer difficulties and complications for the uplifting of the soul (being, as we should say, darkened and hardened by the Fall), wherefore Socrates welcomed death as a form of recovery. This is a true experience, but one that reveals only half the truth and has its place in a much wider context, as we may recognize. It is, indeed, an experience of fact, and is expressed in the late Jewish apocryphal writing, the Wisdom of Solomon, which is certainly influenced by the Hellenistic spirit. 'For a perishable body weighs down the soul, and this earthly tent (*geodes skēnos*) burdens the thoughtful mind (*nous*)' (9:15). In the Latin version: '*Corpus enim, quod corrumpitur, aggravat animam, et terrena inhabitatio deprimit sensum multa cogitantem*'. But this does not yet say anything about the value of the body itself in the whole evolution of the world. If Plato could not do justice to the significance of man's earthly body, that says nothing against his insight into the supersensible by virtue of the special faculty he had of lifting up his soul. Finally, it does not matter whether an idea is 'Platonic' or 'biblical', but if it is 'right'. It is an old experience of mankind that the soul can more or less free itself from the earthly body even before death. Words like 'ecstasy' (standing outside) or 'being out of oneself' indicate such experiences. Paul also knows the experience of being 'out of the body' (2Cor.12:2), as well as the apocalyptist when he says, 'I was in the Spirit' (Rev.1:10; 4:2). In the Old Testament, the prophet, Ezekiel, experienced being out of his body

(3:14; 8:3; 11:1; 40:2). While his body remains in Babylon, he beholds events in distant Jerusalem.

Nor is the Old Testament entirely lacking in indication of an existence after death. The patriarchs are 'gathered in death to their people' (Gen.25:8; 35:29; 49:33). At least in the case of Abraham, the first of the patriarchs to be buried at Hebron, far away from the tombs of his ancestors in Chaldea, it cannot refer only to the common family tomb. We mentioned before the *Sheōl*, the realm of shades corresponding to the Greek *Hades*, where, according to the Old Testament, departed souls have an existence—limited, it is true, but still one from which they could be conjured, albeit by impious means, (Samuel by the witch of Endor, 1Sam.28). At the death of Rachel it is said: 'her soul was departing' (Gen.35:18). When Elijah raised the son of the widow from death 'he stretched himself upon the child three times' and prayed, 'O LORD my God, let this child's soul come into him again' (1Kings,17:21). In the late Jewish period we find in the Second Book of Maccabees, besides the hope of a future resurrection (7:9–23; 12:43–46), the story of the high priest Onias to whom the prophet Jeremiah, long since dead, appears in spiritual glory as intercessor and helper of his oppressed people (15:13–16).

When at Caesarea Philippi the Christ asks who in the opinion of the people the Son of Man is, besides Elijah the name of Jeremiah is also particularly mentioned (Matt.16:14). Ordinary people, therefore, reckoned with the possibility that this long-dead prophet—and perhaps even another of those godly men—was a living spirit and could even appear again in human form. The mention of the name of Jeremiah in the time of the New Testament is in harmony with the passage quoted from Maccabees.

In the Wisdom of Solomon, another of the apocryphal books, we find, probably as a result of Greek influence in the great melting pot of Alexandria, even the idea of *pre-existence*. The soul not only lives on after death—the soul of the righteous one is in the hand of God without pain and in peace (3:1–3), but it was already in existence before birth and found its appropriate earthly body: 'As a child I was by nature well-endowed, and a good soul fell to my lot; or rather, being good, I entered an undefiled body' (8:19–20). Regarding such a passage it is not sufficient that one simply traces its origin in Greek thought. In its encounter with Greek ways of thinking, Judaism, seeking a complete concept of truth, could nevertheless absorb elements of a world picture which complemented the one-sidedness of the Old Testament. The early church therefore included in its biblical canon as of equal value those Hellenistic apocryphal writings which were later excluded by a narrower-minded Judaism.

A whole series of quotations from the Gospels describes a future state of blessedness: 'and sit at table with Abraham, Isaac, and Jacob' (Matt.8:11); 'enter into the joy of your master' (Matt.25:21,23); 'they may receive you into the eternal habitations' (Luke 16:9); 'gather the wheat into my barn' (Matt.13:30); 'the harvest is the close of the age, and the reapers are angels' (Matt.13:39); 'The angels will come out and separate the evil from the righteous' (Matt.13:49); 'the righteous will shine like the sun in the kingdom of their Father' (Matt.13:43). But this all concerns 'the close of the age' just like the contrasting pictures of the 'furnace of fire' (Matt.13:42,50); 'the outer darkness' (Matt.8:12; 22:13; 25:30); men who 'weep and gnash their teeth' (Matt.8:12; 13:42,50; 22:13; 24:51; 25:30); 'the eternal punishment' (Matt. 25:46).

There are, however, also sufficient clear indications in the New Testament of an independent existence of departed souls *between* their dying and that 'close of the age'.

The advocates of the idea that body and soul form one unit are right in stating that the word '*psyche*' in many places in the New Testament means that soul quality which is intimately connected with the body (*bios*). It can therefore occasionally be translated as 'life'; for instance: 'Do not be anxious about your life (*psyche*), what you shall eat or what you shall drink, nor about your body, what you shall put on . . .' (Matt.6:25). There is no doubt that during his incarnation man's soul is immersed to a high degree in his bodily processes. But the soul also has the ability to unite itself on a higher level with the spiritual world. In the saying: 'Do not fear those who kill the body but cannot kill the soul' (Matt.10:28), *psyche* undoubtedly means something *independent of the body*. According to Luke (8:55), at the raising of Jairus's daughter, the spirit that had just left the body returned to it at the call of the Lord. When the young man fell out of the window and lay as if dead, Paul recognized that 'his life is in him' (Acts 20:10). In the parable of the Rich Fool it is said: 'This night your soul is required of you' (Luke 12:20). Christ Himself makes his last prayer in the words of the 31st Psalm (v.5): 'into thy hand I commit my spirit'. Stephen, the first martyr, prayed as he died, 'Lord Jesus, receive my spirit' (Acts 7:59). Already in the magnificat of Mary, 'soul' and 'spirit' are specifically mentioned (Luke 1:46–47). The Letter to the Hebrews speaks of 'the spirits of just men made perfect' (12:23); these spirits of the dead are already alive and active before the resurrection on the Last Day. The first Christians knew that they were surrounded by a 'cloud of witnesses' freed from the body (Heb.12:1). In the Apocalypse, the martyrs who have died are called 'souls' (*psychai*) and the author tells how he sees them 'under the altar' (6:9). Again he uses the word 'souls' (*psychai*) (20:4) for those freed from the body; the martyrs live and reign royally with Christ. Their state is called that of 'the first resurrection'. This is not yet the resurrection of the body—the vision of the final overthrow of death is first described later (20:14)—but the beginning of that resurrection already experienced by the soul in the realm of the dead, as we understand it from Christ's descent into Hades and His words, 'though he dies he lives'. Since Christ's deed, man's existence after death can be entirely different. The expression 'first resurrection' used in the Apocalypse is obviously related to the 'second death' (Rev.2:11; 20:6, 14; 21:8), the languishing in darkness of the departed soul after its separation from the body after the 'first death'. The 'first resurrection' experienced by the martyrs overcomes the death of the soul through the resurrection of the soul. The 'first death' will be overthrown only by the 'second resurrection' which extends even to the body. Between these two references to the *psychai* (6:9 and 20:4), we find repeated visions of the apocalyptist concerning the departed souls of the martyrs (7:9–17; 15:2–4; 19:14), all these still *before* the resurrection of the body.

It should also be remembered that John the Baptist is recognized as the prophet Elijah come again (Matt.11:14; 17:13), Elijah whose ascension the Old Testament describes (2Kings 2:11) and who, moreover, was always felt in Israel to be alive. Elijah appears as a spiritual figure at the Transfiguration of Christ (Matt.17:3), just like Moses, who had died long ago. Both communicate spiritually with Christ and look ahead to the forthcoming event of Golgotha (Luke 9:31). Abraham, too, is living although he died. Christ points out the materialism of the Sadducees by drawing attention to the saying: 'I am the God of Abraham, and the God of Isaac, and the God of Jacob'. God 'is not God of the dead, but of the living' (Matt.22:32). In Luke's version are added the words: 'for all live to him' (20:38). In the story of the beggar Lazarus, Abraham, living in the other world, appears as the special guardian spirit and helper of the Israelites after death (Luke 16:19–31). In John's Gospel, Christ says of Abraham: 'He saw it [my day] and was glad' (8:56). One might think that here, perhaps, Abraham's meeting with Melchizedek was meant, when a ray of light from the approaching age of Christ touched his life. But the context of John's account seems to point in another direction. The argument of the Jews: 'You are not yet fifty years old, and have you seen Abraham?' would be meaningless if they were thinking of something that happened millenniums ago. The Jews were well aware of the time-scale of their history. What do the fifty years mean? Rudolf Steiner once drew attention to the fact that the various stages of man's life each bear within them the corresponding various possibilities of knowing deeper secrets. Apparently the Jews had the idea that a man must have at least seven times seven years behind him to be mature enough to be granted spiritual sight of the Patriarch. It is therefore a matter of the possibility of a meeting in the spirit with Abraham who, like Moses and Elijah, looks with sympathy 'from beyond' at what happens on earth.

The story of Lazarus and the Rich Man (Luke 16:19–31) already mentioned presents a completely different idea from that of 'Total Death'. In the Gospel it is not given as a 'parable', it is rather an event taken from life. Here, with utmost clarity, we are told what happens to departed souls, not after the last resurrection, but shortly after death. Neither the rich man nor Lazarus came to a complete end when their bodies died, but they had very different experiences after death. One death is not the same as another. The phrase about the rich man, 'and was buried', is in strong contrast with the description of Lazarus 'carried by the angels to Abraham's bosom'. Angelic beings, who live in the higher worlds, take the soul and accompany it into that region of the spiritual world to which devout Jews felt themselves drawn through an inner relationship—expressed in the picture of Abraham's bosom. They meet the soul of their forefather and feel sheltered within it. The angels could not as it were 'get at' the rich man who had been immersed in earthly pleasures. It takes quite a time till he comes to awareness, 'lifts up his eyes', and finds himself in a state of painful deprivation. As a result of his earthly life of sensual pleasure, those desires which can be satisfied only by means of the body have eaten into his soul and now torment him with 'burning pain'. He is not in Abraham's bosom but in Hades (Luke 16:23). Yet, on becoming more aware ('he lifted up his eyes'), he was able to see Abraham as the duly appointed guide of his soul, but 'far away'. He looks into a world that is foreign to him. There he also becomes aware of Lazarus. The past life still lives in the memory; people with whom one was together on earth are recognized again. The next step after lifting up his eyes is finding his voice and calling out to Abraham: 'Father Abraham, have mercy upon me,' begging that Lazarus might be sent to him to dip the end of his finger in water and cool his tongue. His tongue—he had totally plunged his soul into the pleasures of a gourmand—now causes his most burning pain. 'I am in anguish in this flame.' Now a spiritual conversation really develops. There is heard the voice of Abraham who lovingly addresses him as 'son', but who has to make plain to him what must inevitably happen. 'Remember'! After death the past life emerges again. '. . . you in your lifetime received your good things.' Now it becomes painfully clear: The lifetime now finished was really 'yours', but you did not use it well. You pursued what you imagined to be 'your' good—worldly pleasures; now you must see that 'your good' is gone with the physical pleasures, leaving behind only a burning sense of deprivation. The 'chasm' that is fixed between Hades and Abraham's bosom is a picture showing that at least for a certain time after death things remain the same as they were at the moment of death. When we are still living on earth we always have the privilege of changing our minds and our ways at any time. After death this possibility of still changing our destiny no longer pertains in this way—(the criminal on the cross was able to give a decisive turn to his destiny at the very last moment).

Destinies are formed on earth; after death their true worth or worthlessness are tasted to the full. As an inexorable consequence, slowly the 'awakening' of the rich man goes on. Even a feeling of love for his fellow creatures arises in his soul in that he remembers his brothers still living on earth whom he would like to warn. But this is not possible either. Here the story breaks off. It is certainly not meant to be a comprehensive study on the life after death, but with profound seriousness it gives in a concrete example a partial picture, a glimpse of what can happen to a person in the other world just after death. The narrative is so accurate, according to occult investigation, in all its details that it should not be dismissed as a casual story adapted to suit the popular taste. The curtain is lowered at a certain point in the story, but the inexorable justice of experiences after death has been shown. It is not said, however, that the anguished deprivation of the rich man should last for ever. There is another indication by Christ that unpleasant experiences after death have to be gone through, but then come to an end. He advises a willingness to put difficult human relationships in order whilst people are still in association with each other—'while you are going with him' (Matt.5:25). Again the importance of life on earth is stressed, for there destiny is made, the points, as it were, are set. If the difficulty is not overcome during a man's lifetime on earth, it will have far-reaching consequences in the higher realms. The matter will be taken before the divine judge who will hand over the guilty to be punished, as Luke (12:58) describes in detail. The sinner fallen into the power of those beings who mete out punishment experiences the loss of his freedom, caused through his evil actions, as 'imprisonment' and has to suffer this state to the end. He 'will never get out' till he has 'paid the very last copper.'

In the *Summa Theologica* of Thomas Aquinas there is a remarkable description of how departed souls reach their 'places'. Thomas says that bodies have a tendency to sink (*gravitas*) as well as to rise (*levitas*) whereby their place is determined. So for departed souls the pull from the higher worlds makes itself felt as 'levity', and the pull from the lower world as 'gravity' according to the quality of the past earthly life. The soul then follows, as it were, the magnetic pull from that supersensible region to which it feels akin, either 'gravitating' or 'levitating' as the case may be (Summa Theol. Suppl. 69.2).

In the Second Letter of Peter, even the word '*exitus*' (in Greek '*exodos*', exit, way out) is used for dying, today often employed in a medical sense, but no longer literally (1:15). The expression means that something does exist which at death goes away and takes its own course. Thus death is also described by Peter as 'putting off my body' (Greek, 'tent') (2Pet.1:14). Despite his hope of metamorphosis of the body through the final resurrection Paul expects after dying (*analyein*) to 'be with Christ' (Phil.1:23). The expression 'to fall asleep', often used for dying, does not contradict such an expectation. 'Falling asleep' has in common with dying the soul's 'slipping out' of the narrow confinement of the body. A person in deep sleep does not hear the sound of the clock because with his soul he is not 'within' the ear, which has not outwardly changed. In sleep, the loosening of the soul from the body is partial, while in death the soul departs completely, also taking with it the delicate life-organism, the etheric forces. The actual process of separation, however, is the same in sleep as in death.

Neither does the 'Total Death' theory find support in John's Gospel, which so strongly stresses the fact that a true higher life can also be gained during earthly life through the initial 'immediate' experiences which are possible. He who believes in the Son '*has* eternal life; he does not come into judgment, but has passed from death to life. Truly, truly, I say to you, the hour is coming, *and now is*, when the dead will hear the voice of the Son of God, and those who hear will live' (5:24–25). Something of the 'and now is' came about at the pool of Beth-zatha for the paralysed man who lay there like a dead man with no longer the will to be healed, and then heard the awakening call: 'Rise ... and walk' (John 5:9). Those wakened by Christ from a state of 'soul death' already have their share in the higher life. The saying that follows about 'all who are in the tombs' and will arise 'to the resurrection of life' or 'to the resurrection of judgment' (5:28,29) points to the final transformation of the body on the Last Day. There is missing here the addition, 'and now is', after the expression, 'the hour is coming'. But the inner experience of resurrection that is possible 'now' definitely excludes a total destruction by death. The final resurrection on the Last Day of 'those who have done good' is resurrection in the full meaning of the word, it is 'the resurrection of life'. The other case of those coming to 'the resurrection of judgment', of separation, surely indicates that at the end of the world, and therewith the end of the possibilities it offers, there faces those who have misused its possibilities during their lives a final, inexorable and uncompromising reckoning. The words about the 'pain of fire' in the synoptic Gospels and the Apocalypse indicate that, once all mere illusion has vanished, the Divine Love asserts itself as the ultimate reality, the 'fire' which Christ would 'throw upon the earth'. 'Who is near me is near the fire' is an apocryphal saying of the Lord. If man lives with this divine element of fire in his innermost being it is bliss for him. But if in his soul he stands aloof, he feels this element of love which is outside him as a permanent reproach, as burning pain.

The passages quoted so far suffice to show that the doctrine of 'Total Death' is not in accord with important biblical statements. *Those who have died do have an existence between death and the Last Day.*

One cannot, however, ignore the fact that the statements and indications related to the subject are very fragmentary. The question was raised at the beginning of this chapter: What lies between death and the Last Day? How will the process of man's becoming Christian (the development, according to Paul, 'to mature manhood, to the measure of the stature of the fulness of Christ' (Eph.4:13)) begun on earth but interrupted by death, continue between death and the Last Day? To this question no comprehensive answer has been found. Partial aspects only have appeared.

This is reflected in the development of Christian thinking, in the history of dogma. The early Christians stood at first under the powerful impression and the dynamic impact of the Resurrection. They were suddenly confronted with something from the far future and the immediacy of the experience made them feel that the Last Day was within easy reach. It can happen, for instance, that at the beginning of a journey the place one is making for is visible in the distance, but as one goes on it may disappear behind forests and mountains though it is gradually being approached. Such a prophetic high-lighting of the distant goal apparently fell to the share of the early Christians in their enthusiastic experiences as they are described in The Acts of the Apostles. A wind from the future was blowing in. We must see in this context, too, the fact that the early Christians expected the end so soon—an expectation for which they have been blamed. There is no doubt they did imagine the Last Day coming soon. They saw the future in that foreshortened perspective often noticeable in connection with prophecies. This says nothing against the truth of prophecies, but it shows that the course of events turns out to be much more complicated and long-lasting than may be understood from the vision, in which long periods of evolution can be compressed. But one should not overlook the fact that the Gospel itself even to some extent excludes this erroneous expectation. Before entering Jerusalem, Christ tells his followers a parable to repress that hectic expectation, 'because he was near to Jerusalem, and because they supposed that the kingdom of God was to appear immediately' (Luke 19:11). In the parable told in the last apocalyptic talk on the Mount of Olives, the virgins who went to meet the bridegroom have to wait a long time 'as the bridegroom was delayed' (Matt.25:5). The same characteristic word, '*chronizein*', used here occurs also in another parable in the talk on the Mount of Olives (Matt.24:48: 'my master is delayed'). And while from the accounts of Matthew and Mark one might gather that the destruction of Jerusalem and the Temple already announces the actual beginning of the end of the world, the report of Luke has kept the insertion: 'until the times (*kairoi*) of the Gentiles are fulfilled' (21:24). Rather than lightly rejecting this expectation of an imminent end as a complete illusion, we should understand that it came about through the bursting of the Resurrection upon the disciples like lightning, so that the future, brightly illuminated, seemed close to them. Attention was spellbound by the final resurrection and consideration of the destinies of departed souls after death stayed in the background.

Only when the early Christians became increasingly aware that they had to adapt themselves to a longer period of time on earth did they begin to form thoughts about the gradually lengthening 'intervening period' between Easter morning and the Last Day. And the theological ideas which developed about this intervening period reflect the fact that the biblical statements are only fragmentary. Thus came the idea that the departed souls would be in a state of sleep till the Last Day (*psychopannychia*). Or it was assumed that immediately after death the soul would be judged and straight away experience bliss or unhappiness until, on the Last Day, the resurrection of the body would be added. Then the question could arise whether the significance of the Last Day would be underrated if it was only to add something to the already existing state of bliss or unhappiness; whether the interest in the great metamorphosis of heaven and earth expected as the end of all would suffer if the soul could already enjoy the beatific vision (*visio beatifica*) of God during the 'intervening period'. In the year 1336, Pope Benedict II solemnly declared (correcting his predecessor, John XXII) that the blessed 'distinctly behold God Himself as He is, Threefold and One', and the souls of the saints in heaven 'behold the Divine Being who clearly and openly reveals Himself to them' (Bull, *Benedictus Deus*). This was reconfirmed at the Council of Florence in 1439. If, then, the *visio beatifica*, the beatific vision of God, is possible already soon after death, the question naturally follows: 'What can the Last Day bring of greater significance than that?' Belief in the resurrection of the body came by tradition, but nobody could tell what its additional value might be. Characteristic of this problem is the sentence in B. Bartmann's (Roman Catholic) *Grundriss der Dogmatik**: 'An increase of bliss after the resurrection is certain; the question is how to explain it'. What is missing is an adequate and exact insight into the various forms of supersensible existence. The different experiences of bliss departed souls can have are pressed into one single, absolutely rigid concept which excludes any thought of there being *stages* in their experience. The establishment of the possibility of a perfect *visio beatifica* already after death means that the resurrection of the body on the Last Day loses its significance. The one-sidedness stemming from Platonism had an effect upon the way in which the experience of bliss by the departed souls was regarded. There is a lack of comprehension of the great additional gift the spiritualized resurrection body gives on the Last Day as the organ that enables the eternal human

* Herder, Freiburg, 1923, p. 566.

individuality to be absolutely itself, though at the same time in communion with all those in the spiritual world, as an independent member of the great community of heaven.

Alternatively, with the notion that our ideas of time might not be applicable to the other world, the attempt was made to place the moment of death and the Last Day side by side. Another question was whether there was a process of purification for the departed soul—a purgatory, a 'purging fire'. Attempts were made, for instance by the Biblicists, to harmonize the various contradictory statements about the other world—Hades, Gehenna, Abraham's bosom, Paradise—in a kind of topography of that world. And now the 'Total Death' theory has recently completely swept aside the idea of the 'intervening period'. 'In any case, the question about the dead cannot be answered otherwise than by reference to death and the Last Day—nothing more. It is wrong to think of anything in between.'* We have seen that this extreme theory has no place in Christianity. The fact remains, however, that the ideas so far developed about the 'intervening existence' are fragmentary. *Here there is a gap in the Christian concept.*

Consideration of the basic events concerning Christ have led us to recognize that within the framework of the unique Descent and Ascent there is no place for reincarnation. It is different with the 'other side' of Christianity—with 'man becoming Christian'. The deed of redemption came about not in heaven but on earth. Man, who lives in an earthly body, is both called upon and able to accept it. It is on earth that man becomes Christian, a process that is interrupted by death. During the life after death, the foregoing life is worked through again and experienced in bliss or pain. But what bridges the gap till the Last Day? Here the idea of reincarnation should be considered seriously. It could well fill the 'eschatological gap'.

* Paul Althaus, *Die letzten Dinge*, Gütersloher Verlagshaus, 9th edition, p. 159.

II
Reincarnation

From Buddha to Lessing

Again and again one meets the prejudice that the teaching of reincarnation is an Indian-Buddhist affair. We already began by citing the example of the Norwegian king, Olaf, to show that the idea of reincarnation was originally much more widespread than in India only. We have also drawn attention to the fact that in the eighteenth century the idea of reincarnation, so long suppressed by the Christian Church, emerged again in western thought.

The most remarkable example is Lessing who, in 1780 in his last-testament-like treatise, *The Education of the Human Race*, seriously considers the question of repeated lives on earth. It is instructive to compare the basic attitude of this treatise with that of Buddhism. To Buddha, reincarnation is a self-evident fact. He does not take it as a mere doctrine but has knowledge of reincarnation through his own spiritual vision. For him, however, it appears in an unfavourable light. He recognizes that life means suffering; he cannot doubt that thereby life itself is 'refuted'. The question is how suffering can be removed. The answer: only by putting an end to life. Today's all-pervasive materialistic thinking would conclude that one has a ready way of putting an end to the misery of life in suicide. Buddha's wisdom was deeper. He knew that in such a case the soul survives with all the innate will to live which simply leads it again into a body. A plant merely cut above ground level grows anew. It must be uprooted. Buddha knew that even if a man feels he is sick of life, nevertheless in deeper unconscious levels of his soul the will to exist still burns as hunger for existence, as desire, as 'thirst'. If this is to come to an end one must work in the depths of the soul with energetic meditation, must tread the path of pain, in order finally to kill the will to live at its root and so find the way to Nirvana. The misfortune of entanglement in bodily existence is thereby cancelled and one is released from the treadmill of reincarnations. Buddha sees the achievement of this end in the characteristic picture of a ruined house. The house means the body. Buddha sees the power which again and again builds the house of the body for man as a real being before him—'the House-builder'. At the end of the path he can speak to him triumphantly: 'Without rest I have wandered through the cycle of many births seeking the House-builder. Painful is this coming to birth again and again. House-builder, you are discovered! Never again will you build the house. Your beams are broken up and the roof of your house fallen in.'

How completely different is the attitude of Lessing! To him the idea of repeated earth lives appears in a favourable light. He does not regard man's individual earthly life as accidental. He consents to his existence and joyfully experiences the possibilities of evolution. He knows the joy of developing and of learning for which one existence on earth does not suffice. History is not meaningless to him but shows a progressive development of human potentialities. As a spiritual community mankind passes through the various stages of culture in a great process of learning. We ourselves have lived in past cultures, carrying their fruits in the still unconscious depths of our souls, forgetful of them for the time being in order to safeguard the impartiality of our present existence, but expecting that what has fallen into oblivion need not therefore be forgotten for ever.

Comparing this concept of repeated earth lives with that of Buddhism one faces a radical reassessment of values. The quantity with the minus sign appears on the other side of the equation with a plus sign. Reincarnation is seen in an entirely new light. Between Buddha and Lessing the Mystery of Golgotha took place. Though Lessing consciously paid tribute to the 'Age of Enlightenment' and could not comprehend the deep mysteries of Christianity, nevertheless he stood in the stream of the purely objective effects of Christ's deed when he spoke so positively about man's existence. The negative attitude, not yet touched by Christian thought, emerges impressively on the western cultural scene in the Buddhist-tinged philosophy of Schopenhauer. There we find his remarkable statement: 'Nothing else can be suggested as the aim of our existence than knowing that it would be better if we did not exist. Yet this is the most important of all truths.'*

Luke's Gospel tells the story of the journey to Emmaus (Luke 24). It shows the relation of Christian and Buddhist thinking. Talking to each other on their way to Emmaus, the two disciples, who on Good Friday had experienced the breakdown of their hopes, sought to cope with the terrible enigma of the Lord's coming to such an end. The Risen One joins them and walks with them, at first unrecognized. He asks for the cause of their distress and then says something that seems like a great rectification of the Buddhist concept of suffering: 'Was it not necessary that the Christ should suffer these things and enter into his glory?' (Luke 24:26). The Christ would not enter into His own specific state of glory without going through the Passion. Holy Week confirmed the truth of Buddhism insofar as suffering is the tenor of earth existence. But this is no longer—as it was with Buddha—the undisputed argument against the value of earthly existence. Suffering reveals its meaning; it is the necessary first step towards the Easter glory. Permeated by this positive attitude to life, Paul can write to the Romans: 'I consider that the sufferings of this present time are not worth comparing with the glory that is to be revealed to us (*apokalyptein*)' (8:18). The Risen One proclaims the Christian truth about suffering while walking with the two disciples. It was indeed truth on a spiritual 'path' that they gained 'on the way'. And as at the end of Buddha's path there stands the final image of the broken-down house, so the way of the Emmaus disciples, which has become their path of knowledge, comes to its end in the house (24:29). In this house the Risen One shares the meal with the disciples, and as He broke bread for them, they knew Him. At the end of the Christian way stands the house of the resurrection body which is connected with the mystery of the Last Supper. It spreads its

* *The World as Will and Idea*, Suppl. to Bk. 4, ch. 48.

light over the Emmaus story. The disciples could have said with Buddha: 'House-builder, you are discovered', but not in the negative sense that with such discovery they would destroy his work. It is not an evil demon who drives man again and again into the fate of reincarnation that is recognized, but Christ Himself who appears as the great builder who builds the house for eternity. In a profoundly symbolic way Jesus of Nazareth was already a carpenter, a *téktōn* (Mark 6:3).

According to Buddha, two concepts play an important role, and that in an entirely negative sense. What must be overcome on the path of inner striving he calls '*Name* and *Form*'. In the *Name* man's ego is reflected; his earthly name represents the eternal name by which God has called him into existence—also the Christian concept. For Buddha the *Name* appears only as the focal point of illusory egoism, the embodiment of empty self-delusion. Broadly speaking, this may be so, but this misuse and contempt of the name is no proof against its original importance. The individuality revealed in the name carries a special form of its own in soul and spirit, just as it does in the body. Again Buddha sees in the individual *Form* only selfishness and personal peculiarities, the bearer of self-delusion. This may also be the case, but for Christians the individual form of the body has its dignity, too, as well as the name, in that the human face, imperfect as it may be, stands for the 'Eternal Countenance'. Finally, Name and Form are the Higher Ego and the Resurrection Body. For all its greatness, Buddhism has no eye for either concept. Buddha lived *before* the Deed of Golgotha. In the 'I am' of the Christ who has become man there sounds the *Name*; in His resurrected body there is revealed the *Form*. By including the Emmaus story in our considerations we neither maintain that the idea of reincarnation already follows from it nor, on the other hand, that Lessing consciously connected his concept with the Resurrection. But the Emmaus story seen in comparison with Buddhism may draw attention to the change that has actually come about through Golgotha and without which the renewed interest in the idea of reincarnation in the Christian west with such an entirely different emphasis cannot be understood.

Rudolf Steiner

Rudolf Steiner's *Anthroposophy*, so often viewed in a really disgracefully superficial manner as an importation from India, will also now be viewed against this background. Rudolf Steiner, born in 1861, realized already as a child that a supersensible world was open to him, which—as he soon noticed—just did not exist for the people around him. Consequently he kept silent about his supersensible experiences until he was forty years old. From the beginning he had a perceptively alert conscience about the matter; he had to ask himself how to relate his supersensible insight to the methods of natural science and the general attitude to knowledge prevalent in the modern world. First he linked his thoughts with the new way of looking at things found in Goethe's endeavours in natural science, till then hardly appreciated, and then proceeded to describe his own epistemology which found its complete expression in *Die Philosophie der Freiheit*, 1894*. So without any reference to 'occult' matter, he built a bridge between modern scientific method and the recognition of the supersensible as it can first of all be grasped through the experience of thinking becoming aware of itself.

Only after the turn of the century, after decades of work, did he break his silence about his supersensible experiences. At first he found an audience only in the Theosophical Society (founded in 1875 by H. P. Blavatsky and H. S. Olcott) of which he was General Secretary from 1902–1912. As already mentioned, he always kept his total independence and, in contrast to usual theosophical teaching, placed the Christ-Event as the centre-point of world history. He recognized in the history of mankind the continuing development of ego-consciousness which at first caused the loss of ancient clairvoyance, but enables man to receive Christ as his higher ego (what Novalis called 'The Ego of egos') and so find access in a new way to the spiritual world of his origin. In 1913 Rudolf Steiner founded the Anthroposophical Society. Some of his basic books are:

* First published in English as *The Philosophy of Spiritual Activity*. Latest English edition with the title *The Philosophy of Freedom*, Rudolf Steiner Press, London, 1964.

Rudolf Steiner

Wie erlangt man Erkenntnisse der höheren Welten? (1904), *Theosophie* (1904), *Die Geheimwissenschaft im Umriss* (1910)*.

In the two last named books, reincarnation is also considered in principle and in general, not in the vague form of divinations, dreams or mere speculative reflections, but as the result of conscientious and profound spiritual investigation, so formulated that it can make its way into the modern climate of opinion. This is based upon a description of *what man's being really comprises.* Current anthropology approaches the nature of man in a very limited way. To do it justice, methods of investigation of a higher order must be used, of which a precise account is given. As the supersensible part closest to man's physical body there appears the life-organism, the 'etheric body', which the plants also have. The 'astral body' is the bearer of the soul forces and is also present in animals. Then, within the human soul there comes to life what makes man an individual, his own 'ego', the spiritual nucleus that comes from eternity and passes through numerous lives on earth. At first this ego is still largely hidden because of its physical sheaths. In the physical, etheric and astral bodies heredity is at work. It is by no means denied—though strictly speaking it proves no more than that 'the stone which falls into water gets wet'—that when the ego incarnates in a certain family it covers itself with the sheaths characteristic of that family. Nevertheless it remains basically a quite individual being deriving nothing from heredity. As such it is not condemned to submerge itself completely in the inherited sheaths. The ego can work on the gifts of heredity and to a certain extent transform them and adapt itself to them.

The anthroposophical exposition of reincarnation cannot be reproached with overlooking the very intimate relationship of soul and body and assuming a much more distant association (rather on the analogy of moving from one furnished room to another and never really settling anywhere). Involvement in the hereditary character of a particular family is not accidental. The soul nearing incarnation has already taken up a relationship with the line of heredity concerned, seeking proper conditions for itself and guided in the 'choice of parents' by the profound

* *Knowledge of the Higher Worlds. How is it achieved? Theosophy* and *Occult Science—an Outline*, Rudolf Steiner Press, London, 1976, 1973 and 1972.

wisdom of destiny. It also brings its own etheric and soul forces. If one wants to trace the derivation of this ego, it should not be from ancestors but 'from itself' insofar as it came here from earlier attempts at self-realization in previous lives on earth. Here Rudolf Steiner draws attention to the fact that man—and man alone—has a 'biography', and to the special 'spiritual form' that belongs uniquely to each one and reflects its history and formation in earlier incarnations. If by contemplating a man's destiny one has the impression from what has just happened to him, 'this could only happen to *him*' or 'that looks like *him*', one is on the track of his spiritual form and the ego-being that creates his biography. The blows and blessings of destiny have their causes in previous incarnations, but the ego is free to decide how to meet what happens to it as good or bad fortune. It is also free to make 'entirely new starts' and thereby create new consequences, either good or bad.

Human beings whose destinies are connected do not meet only after death but also in subsequent earth lives, according to the conditions they have created. They do not lose each other in the next earth life by being 'someone else'. The ego remains the same. One should only be clear that it exists at a deeper level than all that makes up a person's 'sheaths'. These are not without their significance. Obviously it is not unimportant whether I belong to this or that race, nation, family, class, or even whether I am a man or a woman. In ancient times, when the ego was not so strongly aware of itself, these conditions were of decisive significance. But 'man as such' is superior to all those distinctions. In the first place he is 'man' and endeavours to let attributes of man or woman, English or French, serve accordingly.

Nor does one lose oneself through reincarnation, in the sense of the question once raised by Wilhelm Busch, whether one then '*can still say: I am?*' *Am I still the same* when I reincarnate as another person? On the contrary it should certainly first be asked: 'Can I in any case say: I am?' Is not even *that* 'I am' determined to a large extent through heredity and environment? Is not what I have already made of myself so far, what truly reveals my individuality, only very little? The more the true ego of man develops, the more he becomes himself. The forces that shape his ego remain and go with him; the more they have already been at work, the more like his true self will a man become in the course of an incarnation. Through all the variations of the outer sheaths his 'eternal countenance' will gradually emerge.

According to Rudolf Steiner's description, as a rule centuries lie between separate incarnations, though there are exceptions. Normally, however, man is granted a long time in the spiritual world. Thus the idea of reincarnation has not the hectic character that attaches to the Indian view that after a short time one returns into a mother's womb. It takes some time after death till the completed earth life is evaluated in the eyes of higher beings, in the sight of God. While living on earth, man has the feeling that he faces and assesses his surroundings, but after death the process is reversed. All well-being or pain felt by an excarnated man depends upon the kind of expression with which the eyes of higher beings rest on him. This indeed means judgment. After this judgment, involving a looking back over the past life, has been completed, and all that in the human soul which proves unacceptable in higher realms has been discarded (not without pain and suffering), the spiritual core of man, together with that spiritually inclined part of the soul which is left to him, proceeds to further experiences. He then passes through even higher regions of the spiritual world, insofar as his inner being is related to them, and prepares his next incarnation in communion with the angelic world and human souls akin to him, so that when the time has come, once again he can have in an earthly body such new experiences as cannot be gained in heaven.

An important difference from eastern concepts lies in the fact that Rudolf Steiner explicitly emphasises that the series of incarnations is *by no means endless*. The possibility of living on earth in a human body had a beginning and will have an end. People today, confronted with an environment spoiled by our civilization, have gradually become aware that their further existence on earth in these particular conditions is by no means a matter of course. Even if some fatal consequences already threatening man's existence could still to some extent be averted, the time will finally come when human incarnations on earth are no longer possible. Thus man, facing his task of becoming 'Man'—to a great extent not yet achieved—has no time to lose. The objection cannot be raised that the idea of reincarnation would weaken man's conscience and slacken his striving. The anthroposophical concept of reincarnation quite removes the basis for such an irresponsible attitude as 'after us, the flood' or 'if not today, then perhaps tomorrow'. The responsibility which is connected for man with each incarnation comes to light in full solemnity. The understanding that the ego is to develop toward freedom and ripen in self-chosen responsibility renders groundless the objection that the idea of reincarnation entails that of an automatic evolution. Anthroposophy does not speak about evolution in the often naïve manner of the nineteenth century when people were deeply impressed by scientific discoveries. Evolution in the anthroposophical sense has many aspects. Consideration of the reality shows how again and again evolution includes set-backs, how new achievements are often gained at the cost of earlier faculties, how sometimes 'going backward' can mean 'going forward'. The passing through repeated lives on earth, where one is confronted with the negative results of one's own ill deeds, and the experience of judgment after each death are no guarantee that a person's condition is bound to improve from one incarnation to another. This, of course, is possible but man must co-operate in his becoming Man. As a consequence of his attitude, his condition can even deteriorate. So reincarnation is by no means identical with 'rebirth'. When the incarnations have come to an end, the judgments there have been after each death are indeed followed by a Last Judgment, resulting in a division of mankind between those who have made good use of their lives on earth and those who have slighted the chances offered them. Lastly it will be decisive whether Christ has been received by man or not. Without accepting what has entered into the evolution of mankind through Christ, man cannot fulfil his task of becoming Man. Becoming Man will be recognized more and more as identical with becoming Christian (not meant, of course, in the narrow sense of a religious confession). It was not an interest in Christian apologetics that led Rudolf Steiner to his Christological statements. In pursuit of his exact spiritual investigation he was confronted by the supersensible fact on which Christianity is based. To see Christ in this way also throws a new light on the teaching of karma. The word 'karma' in ancient Indian philosophy means the connection of cause and effect stretching from one incarnation to another. The law of sowing and reaping ('Whatever a man sows, that he will also reap.' Gal.6:7) is valid even from incarnation to incarnation. The deeds and sufferings of an incarnation carried through purely spiritual realms, without contact with the material world, call forth related effects in the next incarnation. The more man's true ego, destined to create in freedom, begins to work, the more (besides the aspect of sowing and reaping) new faculties can begin to be developed, new threads be drawn into his existence. What is brought down from higher realms as a creative impulse, as 'love from above', does not overturn the logic of karma but adds something to the balance sheet of destiny whereby the result is changed.

This is true in the highest sense in regard to Christ Himself. He brings as we have said *Himself*, and, as a new factor coming in, changes the destiny of all mankind. Such a concept as 'the sin of the world' carried by the Lamb of God presupposes the idea of karma. The misdeeds of mankind are a reality in the spiritual world. They exist as a harmful power in the unseen world. A man can make good again always only part of his misdeeds. Out of deep repentance he can even become a saint. If circumstances allow, he can do so much good to the victim of his crime as really to compensate for it, if not in this life, then in a following one. But it would be superficial to think that this is all that should be done. All such 'making good' does not remove from the world the fact that evil has nevertheless been done and that through its actually happening the whole condition of the world has been changed. Man always sins 'beyond his means'. He gets into debt beyond the scope of his ability to repay. The results of Rudolf Steiner's investigations in this regard are in harmony with biblical statements. That third dimension of the evil deed, which harms not only the evil doer himself and his victim, but as it were breaks through into the unseen world of spirit, comes to expression in Psalm 51 when the one who prays to God says: 'Against thee, thee only, have I sinned' (v.4). Likewise in the words of the Prodigal Son who says to his father: 'I have sinned against heaven . . .'; only then follows, 'and before you' (Luke 15:18,21).

All that goes beyond man's ability to compensate gathers

together like an ominous cloud as 'the sin of the world'. Mankind is lost unless a being of a higher order, even the highest, comes to its rescue, one who has—if one may so express it—a much greater radius of action than man, one who has the power to cope with that harmful element. This is Christ as the 'Lamb of God'. Through becoming man he makes Himself one with mankind. In that He 'became flesh' even to the extent of dying, he created the means whereby he could 'approach' the man-made world-sin. Christ must suffer because 'the sin of the world' is real. But He accepts this suffering in His freely-made sacrifice. For every other human being it is true that 'the wages of sin is death'. For Christ it is different. His death has quite another significance. When a sinful man dies the 'fruit of his suffering' is entirely used up for the expiation of his own sins, but the fruit of Christ's suffering benefits all mankind. Since one can rely on the law of karma—sowing and reaping—one may speak of the redeeming power of the death of Christ, which, as 'love from above' infuses into the balance-sheet of mankind's destiny the additional, new factor that transforms the final result. In his cycle of lectures on *Christ and the Human Soul* (Norrköping, July 1914), Rudolf Steiner expounded the harmony between 'grace' and the idea of karma rightly understood.

So, too, the objection is irrelevant that the doctrine of reincarnation, in considering the chance for moral regeneration and expiation, excludes grace by relying on 'self-redemption'. Rudolf Steiner made it quite clear that all human striving and regeneration—indispensable as it is—would fall short without Christ and His sacrifice.

Knowledge of Man

When in 1912 Rudolf Steiner introduced the name 'Anthroposophy' instead of 'Theosophy', chiefly used till then, he did not mean to emphasize what concerned man at the expense of what concerned the divine as has been the case in certain kinds of Humanism. It was much rather to give the impression that in our twentieth century an important *new step in becoming conscious of his own being* has become possible for man: a decisive broadening of man's knowledge of himself. The concept of Man, the '*humanum*', now acquires entirely new supersensible dimensions. Thus it is possible to recognize the importance of the Christ Being for our truly becoming Man. In this way, for the first time in human consciousness, higher Humanism and Christianity can be seen as one.

In the great pre-Christian cultures the vision of divine creative realms greatly outshone man's awareness of his own being. The awareness that 'I am' still slumbered for the most part. Christ could not come till 'the time was fulfilled', before man had at least some awareness of his ego-nature. This came about in the time of the Graeco-Latin culture. Already in the second century B.C., a distinct 'humanism' begins to be articulate for the first time when Roman and Greek personalities meet on a purely human basis, regardless of national barriers. This happened in the circle that formed round the young Scipio, to which Polybius, a prisoner deported from Greece under civil law, also belonged. The Stoic, Panaitios, and the comic dramatist, Terence, a liberated slave, also joined that circle. A striving after the purely human was in the air at that time. Terence had an unheard of success in the theatre when in his *Heautontimorumenos* he let old Chremes say, in a not even particularly sententious way: '*Homo sum, humani nihil a me alienum puto*' (I,1:25). 'I am human and count nothing human alien to me'. Even half a millennium later the Church Father, Augustine, knows of the impact of that sentence. 'This sentence, as we are told, was even applauded in a theatre full of foolish and uneducated people' (letter to Macedonius). Via the Stoic, Poseidonius, '*humanitas*' then finds its way to Cicero (106–43 B.C.). R. Reitzenstein* says that the Greek language had

* *Werden und Wesen der Humanität im Altertum*, Strasbourg, 1907.

not yet found a proper word for it, 'even the idea itself was not yet developed. Only among Romans we find again and again words like "true man" and "humanity", *humanus* and *humanitas*, . . . The "*homo humanus*" was, in a certain circle, deliberately placed in opposition to the "*homo Romanus*" that Cato called for.' The Greek word, '*philanthropia*', had not yet this specific feeling. So what is meant in the New Testament in regard to 'humanity' (*humanitas*) is, exceptionally, clearer in the Latin translation than in the original Greek text. Luke reports in the Acts of the Apostles how the centurion, Julius, treated the prisoner, Paul, *humane* (27:3) and praises the Maltese (called barbarians because of their Semitic language) for their unusual *humanitas* to the shipwrecked (28:2). Paul, in his Letter to Titus (3:4), speaks significantly of God's *humanitas* that appeared through Christ—'loving kindness of God'. One might be inclined to see in this growing feeling for *humanitas* by the ancients one of the environmental factors which produced Christianity. Yet, if one is able to acknowledge in the Christ Being's approach to incarnation an objective spiritual process, one might consider such phenomena as the emergence of *humanitas* rather on the analogy of the redness of dawn, which does not cause the sunrise but, on the contrary, is caused by it. The effect can precede the cause.

Seneca, Paul's contemporary, makes the magnificent statement: '*Homo res sacra homini*', 'Man is a sacred concern for man'. And Seneca was certainly no Christian. We face the fact that the dawning 'humanism' and Christianity go *side by side*. Early Christians could not fully comprehend that in Christ-Jesus the creative archetype, *Humanum*, had truly appeared. They did not see the link between '*Ecce homo*' (John 19:5) and '*humanitas*'. Pilate was probably not aware of just what he expressed by those words, but at that moment he was the interpreter of the world's history. The 'humanists' had the ideal, the Christians the reality, though they were not fully aware of it. Even the 'I am' motif so dominant in St. John's Gospel has so far in the whole history of Christian thought been taken only in the obvious sense of an ordinary personal statement, not in its immense and principal meaning as the revelation of the profoundest mystery concerning man, who is finally destined also to be able to say, 'I am'. It is also a remarkable fact that in the Old Testament the great original description of man in Genesis (1:27) as 'the image of God' stands like a solitary peak, alone. Except in a very few passages (Gen.5:1; 9:6; Ps.8:5; 82:6; Ecclus.17:3) there is no further reference to this Magna Charta of humanity in the Old Testament. Human consciousness had simply still not come anywhere near this sublime inspiration. Then the Christian church, as far as possible, dogmatically laid down the truth of God's becoming Man in Christ Jesus without being really aware about the consequence this 'becoming Man' has for the '*humanum*'.

When the theatre-goers applauded Terence's saying about man, it was certainly in the first place on the basis of the comradeship that unites all who are born human and tolerantly understand what is human, even 'all too human'. Awareness of the deficiencies and dangers of human existence on earth is certainly an integral part of the '*humanum*'. But through Christ's entering human existence and really 'as man' experiencing an earthly destiny, in which he transformed divine powers into human faculties, the '*humanum*' has *undergone an expansion*. At Easter Christ rose from the grave not only as God, but as Man. The '*Ecce homo*' is also true of the One who has risen and ascended to heaven. What then happened to one human being belongs ever since potentially to all men. To the whole idea of the '*humanum*' belong not only weakness and frailty but also what overcomes them: resurrection and ascension. Theodore Haubach (who was put to death in Plötzensee on 3rd January, 1945) had a feeling for it: 'The more I try to penetrate the hidden wisdom of both Testaments, the more I am urged to think that in the last centuries an essential element of the Divine message has become obscured, namely, that man is not only fallen, sinful, small and miserable, but on the other hand capable of participating in the Divine to an extent which our decadent age on the whole no longer understands' (6 July 1944).

The humanism that followed on after the Graeco-Roman period always, with a few exceptions, continued as a parallel development with Christianity; there was even at times a certain tension between them, humanism being alien if not hostile to Christianity. This was the case at the time of the Renaissance when the profounder intellects examined the ancient mysteries, while others found their main ideal in writing an elegant Latin in the style of Cicero. Pico della Mirandola sought a harmony. Then followed the wave of humanism under the aegis of German idealism. Goethe came close to making a connection between humanism and Christianity; in his large-scale poem, *Die Geheimnisse*, the central figure is named Humanus, and the sign of the Rose Cross indicates Christian esotericism—but the poem remained a fragment. The 'pure humanity' which 'atones for all human frailty' was not yet actually recognized in Christ. What broke out as materialism after Goethe's death made 'humanity' its motto, taking it as a substitute for Christianity, which was imagined to have to come to an end. The statement of the great physician, Virchow, is typical: 'The basis of humanism is natural science, and its true expression anthropology.'* Regarding anthropology based on natural science, which does not get to grips with the true 'Anthropos', it is understandable that present theology disfavours the word 'humanism' and tries to keep the ideas of Christianity and Humanism quite separate, just as, on the other side, Humanism is ranged against Christianity.

A mere anthropology like Virchow's cannot do justice to its object; only an anthropo-sophia which takes account of higher faculties of cognition gains a true picture of Man. As Anthroposophy describes it, the nature of man in the differentiation of its sheaths—physical, etheric and astral—which surround the ego, is not something static and fixed, but dynamic and in constant motion. The real ego-nucleus wakes increasingly to self-awareness and accordingly increasingly transforms those sheaths to make them completely its own. Thus begins the gradual building up of man's higher spiritual nature. When this metamorphosis comes to an end, the final point is reached of resurrection and ascension—but only if Christ and 'the power of his resurrection' (Phil.3:10) have been accepted, and the might of the adversaries threatening the true nature of man overthrown. The Godhead has, as it were, taken the risk of leaving man free. Man's future is open, on the one hand for a

* R. Virchow, *Gesammelte Abhandlungen zur wissenschaftlichen Medizin*, Frankfurt a.M., 1856. Compare Gerhard Hiltner, *Rudolf Virchow*, Verlag Freies Geistesleben, Stuttgart, 1970.

terrible disaster, on the other for the continued development of the '*humanum*' towards resurrection and ascension through the union with Christ. Anthroposophy has therefore brought Humanism and Christianity together whereas hitherto in the history of Christendom, owing to prejudices on both sides, they have run only parallel with each other. The name, 'Anthroposophy', itself expresses this new step in man's growing self-awareness. Accordingly the Communion Service of The Christian Community is called 'The Act of Consecration of Man' (*Die Menschenweihehandlung*), a name never before used in the history of Christian liturgy. Just as little as Anthroposophy means excluding 'Theo-sophy' does The Act of Consecration of Man imply opposition to the idea of 'Divine Service'. It just says concretely that we serve God by helping Him to realize His plan for mankind, and this comes about through our connection with Christ. Essentially, the Christian Mystery of Man is contained in the Bible, but has not yet fully emerged in man's consciousness.

A wisdom that recognizes the '*humanum*' as capable of spiritual development and at the same time sees the Christ as the fulfiller of this hope for the future also leads to the recognition of repeated earth lives. Christ is both 'gift' and 'task' for mankind. Just as Lessing's joy in learning and developing allowed him eagerly to anticipate further lives on earth, so, as a result of awakened insight into the mystery of mankind and Christ, there lives a conscious joy in learning and developing in Christians who feel that it is by the grace of God that they are granted not only a single life on earth 'to draw from the fulness of Christ'.

The dream-like consciousness of pre-Christian times accepted the idea of repeated lives on earth as an instinctively known fact. It was possible to suppose that this repetition just continued with no beginning and no end. Certain supersensible impressions, obtained perhaps in visions of departed souls experiencing the power of their own desires after death, could lead to the misunderstanding that even incarnations in animals were possible for the soul of man. Moreover, the impressions a man received of his ancestors living on in supersensible regions could be misinterpreted as his own previous incarnations. Therefore, since man had to wake himself up on earth from the old, often already decadent dreams of the divine, it was meaningful that for a time the depths of the supersensible world were obscured and all light concentrated on the current life on earth. As the higher realms disappeared from view in a 'Twilight of the Gods', so did the prospect of numerous incarnations. Not before man, as an independent and responsible being on earth, freely accepts Christ can he gradually be guided to a new, and now much more conscious increase of awareness of the higher realms and of repeated lives on earth. While the orient was specially gifted in observing the rhythmically recurring *cycles of time*, the Old Testament developed, for the first time on a grand scale, the feeling for the *linear* structure of history. There we find a direct movement forward from a beginning to an end. Only such a sense of history, which knows of the beginning and the end, is able to grasp the uniqueness of the Mystery of Golgotha as the central point in all history.

When the Christian brought up with the biblical outlook is really filled with a sense of the importance of this linear plan of history, he can then proceed to attain to the truth of the repeated cycles of time without sacrificing the linear sense of direction. This would result in something like the image of a *spiral*, which has the characteristic of cycles and yet as a whole moves forward in one direction. In this respect, Goethe says at the end of the eighth book of *Dichtung und Wahrheit* 'that while on the one hand we are forced to be centred in ourselves, on the other we do not neglect, in rhythmic alternation, to reach beyond ourselves'. Such a rhythm between man's being centred in himself during an incarnation and his reaching beyond himself in one of the spiritual realms after death is revealed in the anthroposophical exposition of reincarnation. Through those cycles, however, the whole moves towards its end. In this way, from one cycle to another respectively, what is heavenly can gradually be brought down to earth, and what on earth is ready for heaven be gradually borne upwards. What separated at the creation of the world into 'Heaven' and 'Earth' is then free to be reunited, as the Apocalypse describes, in the 'Marriage of the Lamb', in the union of a 'New Heaven' and a 'New Earth'.

We have described the links between man's being, Christ's

action, and reincarnation so fully in order to show that the idea of reincarnation as Rudolf Steiner presents it is not a matter of some special occult doctrine but something that is *an organic part of the great Christian world picture.* This idea does indeed fill the 'gap' we pointed out when considering Christian eschatology, the teaching of the 'last things'. Once more we emphasize that Rudolf Steiner's researches were not carried out with the special intention of filling that gap. But since the result of his spiritual investigation is now available, we cannot help stating that thereby the gap between man's death and the Last Day is closed. Thereby also another difficulty disappears, one perhaps hardly noticed by the early Christians, which originates in the very uniqueness of Christ's deed. Christianity would no longer be Christianity if it in any way diminished its *claim to be absolute* in the sense expressed by Peter: 'There is salvation in no one else' (Acts 4:12). In places where the history of religion is studied and dialogue with people of other religions sought, such a statement might seem fanatical and narrow-minded. Anthroposophy is able to show how, in many different ways, all religions are based upon original experience of higher worlds. One can see quite clearly and in detail that God has not let Himself 'remain unwitnessed'. It can also be seen that in the ancient religions there are more or less distinct connections with the forthcoming Christ-Mystery. Through acquaintance with the concepts of Imagination and Inspiration, it is possible to do justice to the truth contained in the myths and rites of the pagan world. If the idea of repeated earth lives is accepted, the fact that people living before the time of Christ, and those who have since held themselves aloof from Christianity, did not yet consciously accept Christ, appears in a different light. *Just as the whole world-concept of Christianity finds its completion in the light of reincarnation, so the meaning of reincarnation first becomes completely evident through the orientation toward the central and unique deed of Christ.*

We now turn to the question of how this idea of reincarnation is related to certain statements in the Bible, in particular to the eschatological texts of the New Testament.

III
Reincarnation and the Bible

Old and New Testament

It may be because of the emphasis on the linear structure of history in the Old Testament that there is hardly any mention of repeated earth lives. In his essay on reincarnation, Lessing presents the idea of mankind's 'education'. The way in which he speaks about the Old and New Testaments as 'elementary books' is strongly tinged by the rationalism dominant at that time, but the basic concept of 'education' is absolutely in harmony with Paul, who sees the law of the Old Testament as the custodian, *paidagōgos*, leading us toward Christ, at whose coming 'we are no longer under a custodian' (Gal.3:25). So, according to Paul, the education can be connected with a certain one-sidedness which may be overcome by the onset of Christian development. In a similar way, the Old Testament as a whole can be seen as a teacher primarily concerned with sharpening the awareness of the linear nature of events who therefore, for pedagogical reasons, obscured for a certain period the wider perspective of recurring rhythms.

Some have wanted to find an indication of reincarnation in the words of the ninetieth Psalm (v.3): 'Turn back, O children of men!'—but unjustifiably. The original text either means the return of men who have died, whereby, according to Ecclesiastes (12:7), 'the dust returns to the earth as it was, and the spirit returns to God who gave it', or it might refer to new people being born: 'A generation goes, and a generation comes' (Eccles.1:4).

On the other hand, however, there *is* significance in the prophecy that concludes the last book of the prophets (Mal. 4:5): 'Behold, I will send you Elijah the prophet before the great and terrible day of the LORD comes'. This is as much as to say that a return to a new life on earth is in principle possible, even if perhaps it is an exception. Nevertheless, it gave the Old Testament line of study a starting point for the idea of reincarnation, which plays a certain role in the Jewish secret religious philosophy, most remarkably in the cabbalistic school of Lurija (1534–72) in Safed.*

Through the reincarnation of Elijah in John the Baptist, the Old Testament is absolutely historically bound to the New Testament. In the New Testament, too, the 'pedagogic' obscuring of the wider perspective continues. With the example of Elijah-John, however, the principle of reincarnation has been specifically stated by Christ Himself. The fact that, according to John's Gospel, John the Baptist answered the question, 'Are you Elijah?' with 'I am not' says no more than that he himself is not aware of it (John 1:21). This denial, by the way, has a subtle difference in the way it is formulated from his previous denial when asked, 'Who are you?' (1:19). There the answer is unmistakably clear: 'I am not the Christ (*Ego ouk eimi*)'. Emphasis is given to the 'I' preceding the 'am'. 'My ego is not identical with Christ's ego.' To the question: 'Are you Elijah?' John answers only, '*ouk eimi*'—'am not'. In John's Gospel, in which the *ego eimi* motif plays such an important part, the '*ouk eimi*' (without '*ego*') affords a significant contrast. 'Am not'—this expression, significantly repeated, is used by John for Peter's denial (18:17,25) (otherwise only once, by Luke, 22:58). Peter is not in full possession of his ego-consciousness. John the Baptist's 'Am not' has a different background, but similarly contrasts with the 'I am' of Christ. In this connection Friedrich Rittelmeyer may be quoted: 'The Baptist's saying, "I am not," apart from the immediate meaning of the words, may stress the contrary of the "I am" which from that time is constantly spoken by Christ in John's gospel. So that John—whether consciously

* See Gershorm G. Scholem, *Major Trends in Jewish Mysticism*, Schocken Books, New York, 1954, pp. 281–285.

or not—leads one away from his ego, to the ego which now comes into the forefront. I, in my human personality, will be nothing but a voice calling for Christ, calling on behalf of Christ!'* Since the angel who announces John's birth to Zachariah speaks only of 'the spirit and power of Elijah' in which John 'will go before' the Lord (Luke 1:17), one could take that as a general comparison. But the direct identification is made later by Christ: 'He is Elijah' (Matt.11:14). It is striking that this statement is preceded by the words, 'and if you are willing to accept it'. Thus the truth about reincarnation is declared with a certain caution, a certain sensitive consideration for the individual freedom of the hearer, who should not be overwhelmed by an authoritative statement. The disciples can live for a while with this dictum, heard so far only once, without having hastily to commit themselves to a dogmatic 'Yes' or 'No'. Later comes the moment when the truth, presented to the disciples so unauthoritatively, 'dawns' in their souls. This happens on their descent from the mountain of the Transfiguration: 'Then the disciples understood that he was speaking to them of John the Baptist' (Matt.17:13) when he answered their question about Elijah. Here one can have the impression that with this unique and great example of reincarnation in the New Testament a paradigm is given for the proper Christian way in which the contents of supersensible knowledge should be conveyed to mankind in the future: not by means of authoritative dogma or persuasion, but through a presentation that leaves the hearer entirely free—'if you are willing to accept it'.

As an appeal for purely voluntary attention, for profound individual deliberation, the sentence with which Christ follows His saying about Elijah-John is on the same lines: 'He who has ears to hear, let him hear' (Matt.11:15). This sentence is familiar to all readers of the Bible, though they are not always clear about where it occurs. It is not without importance that it appears for the first time just at the place where Christ reveals the secret of Elijah-John. Then Matthew, who frequently includes particular arrangements of numbers in his Gospel, brings it in twice more, thus making a threefold pattern. These

* Friedrich Rittelmeyer, *Reincarnation*, The Christian Community, London, *c.* 1931 (undated), p. 76.

two other places are Matthew 13:9 and 13:43, both in connection with Matthew's great series of parables (the seven parables 'beside the lake'). Matthew 13:9 is the conclusion of the parable of the Sower, describing the different results for the seed on different soils: what fell on good soil 'brought forth grain, some a hundredfold, some sixty, some thirty. He who has ears, let him hear.' Matthew 13:43 concludes the interpretation of the parable of the Weeds of the Field. At the 'close of the age' (*synteleia*) (13:39) 'the righteous will shine like the sun in the kingdom of their Father. He who has ears, let him hear.' Through this threefold pattern, these passages in Matthew's Gospel are connected with each other: the fact of a reincarnation, the possibility of growing and bringing forth fruit, and the final transfiguration to a glory like the sun.*

Is not reincarnation also mentioned in the New Testament, though indirectly, in John's narrative of the Man Born Blind? The disciples' question whether in this case he or his parents had sinned that he was punished by being born blind seems to indicate an assumpton on their part that 'he himself' could have caused this by his sins in an earlier incarnation. In this respect one must nevertheless take into consideration that there were also at that time Jewish concepts which would have allowed the possibility of the blindness being a result of sins simply in a pre-existence of the soul before birth. But one should not assume from Christ's negative response, 'It was not that this man sinned, or his parents' (John 9:3), His rejection of reincarnation in principle. The negative concerns only this special case, which was different. The possibility that a person's own sin can be involved in being born blind is not, in principle, excluded. At all events, Christ's answer makes an important contribution to the question of destiny, of karma. Just as nowadays one immediately thinks of India when reincarnation is mentioned, so one is also inclined to consider the law of destiny only in its

* Mark and Luke have this formula only at the end of the parable of the Sower, then each once more: Mark after the saying: 'For there is nothing hid, except to be made manifest' (4:22), Luke after the saying about the salt that has lost its taste (14:35). All these passages have a certain apocalyptic element in common. Besides the Gospels, this significant formula is characteristically used in the Apocalypse of John seven times: 'He who has an ear, let him hear what the Spirit says to the churches', at the end of each of the letters to the seven churches (Rev. 2 and 3). It comes once more (13:9) at the rising of the beast out of the sea: 'If any one has an ear, let him hear'.

Indian form. Wherever reincarnation is in question there necessarily follows the idea that the lives on earth are related to each other, and that something like the law of cause and effect must be at work. What Paul first declared as a general truth: 'Whatever a man sows, that he will also reap' (Gal.6:7), also expresses the fundamental law of karma. But even here, an explanation exclusive of Christianity could not do full justice to the facts. Karma then appears as an automatic mechanism for dealing out punishment. Misfortune in one life could be seen only from the angle of punishment for sin in a previous life. But that is only *one* of the possibilities to be considered. It is in this sense that Christ says to the one He healed at the pool of Beth-zatha: 'See, you are well! Sin no more, that nothing worse befall you' (John 5:14). In the ancient doctrine of karma this law was rightly recognized as also working in repeated earth lives. Nevertheless, there is the other possibility—and this was strongly emphasized by Rudolf Steiner—that an impediment, a negative element in an incarnation, is actually *sought* by the incarnating soul without its being a necessary punishment, just in order, perhaps, to gather strength from the hindrance and to develop powers of conquest through the struggle for the sake of a far future. This could indeed be the case with undeserved suffering, while deserved suffering atones for the past.* This possibility of suffering misfortune when guiltless for the sake of a future good is recognized by Christ in the case of the man born blind. 'It was not that this man sinned, or his parents, but that the works of God might be made manifest in him.' Both aspects—John 5:14 as well as 9:3—would be valid from the point of view of reincarnation, and only so gain their full meaning.

Something from the Letter to the Hebrews should also be mentioned which is often carelessly quoted as a negation of the idea of reincarnation: 'And just as it is appointed for men to die once, and after that comes judgment' (9:27). The text continues: 'so Christ, having been offered once to bear the sins of many, will appear a second time'. It is the Letter to the Hebrews which again and again uses the word 'once' (*hapax* or *ephapax*) in relation to the deed of Christ in order to make it quite clear that Christ made the descent into the sphere of death, into *sarx*,

* Compare pp. 67–68.

through Golgotha once and for all, and that His 'coming again' will be a spiritual event occurring under entirely different conditions. The idea of death is here used as indicative of something irrevocable and decisive that concludes a man's life on earth and happens in the course of it only *once*. A mortal man is thereby able to understand just what in the highest sense is meant by 'once' in relation to Christ's deed. Repeated earth lives are certainly not thought of in the Letter to the Hebrews any more than elsewhere in the New Testament. The one death that definitely ends a man's life on earth is brought in as a point of comparison. This uniqueness of the experience of death would not be affected by thoughts of reincarnation. As a particular person, a man dies only once. In a following incarnation, the eternal individuality that goes through all of them builds up another person, through which it 'sounds' (*per-sonat*).* But death is something that happens *once* to each person. After that—*judgment*. This would also be affirmed from the point of view of reincarnation. Death is followed by the experience of the sternest trials. Besides, the original text of that Letter to the Hebrews does not say 'the judgment', but only 'judgment' (*krisis*). There is indeed also in the New Testament the concept of a Last Judgment but that does not exclude 'judgment' being experienced 'already now' in each case after death. There are also moments even in earthly life when one can be profoundly shaken by the experience of a 'judgment'. It meant judgment for Peter when he said to Christ: 'Depart from me, for I am a sinful man, O Lord' (Luke 5:8). Thus, this sentence from the Letter to the Hebrews contains nothing that would stand in the way of the possibility of repeated lives on earth. But how is it with the other eschatological passages of the New Testament? What do they look like if the idea of reincarnation is brought into the picture?

* The word comes from the Latin '*persona*', an actor's mask. *Trans.*

The Eschatology of the Discourse on the Mount of Olives and of Paul's First Letter to the Thessalonians

In the chapter 'Between Death and the Last Day' we took pains to come to a deeper understanding of the first Christians' feeling of the imminence of the Last Day. Through the event of Easter the remotest future was lit up as if it was already present. A wind from the future blew into earliest Christianity. This is why they could not yet really give their minds to the long distance which separates Easter Day from the Last Day for mankind. So for the first Christians the end of the world was imminent, in spite of certain words of Christ to the contrary (see p. 55). Such indications of a long intervening period were disregarded, while visions of spiritual events were misunderstood and wrongly taken to refer to events on earth.

The Mount of Olives apocalypse begins with Christ leaving the Temple with his disciples for the Mount of Olives, probably on the evening of the day of the great disputes. Looking westward, He sees the Temple opposite in all its splendour. Faced by that building, the disciples exclaim in admiration. Christ beholds with prophetic foresight the destruction which was to become terrible reality in the year 70. 'There will not be left here one stone upon another, that will not be thrown down' (Matt.24:2). But this foreseeing of the year 70 is just the beginning of a much wider-reaching prophecy which the destruction of the Temple set in train. The historic event of the year 70 must denfiitely not be regarded, in Lessing's sense, as an 'accidental historical event'. It belongs to a higher order of events which are truly symbolic. The destruction of the Temple is an historic 'rune', one of those events that veils a greater reality. For the faithful of old, the Temple was the embodiment of the words 'on earth as it is in heaven'. In the Old Testament the setting up of the Mosaic tabernacle, which preceded the building of the Temple, is described on the analogy of God's creation of the world in six days,* the same

* cf. Rudolf Frieling, *Bibelstudien*, 'Der Bau der Stiftshütte und der Weltenbau' p. 41, Verlag Urachhaus, Stuttgart, 1963.

words being used for its completion and for the completion of the world's creation (Gen.1:31; 2:1; Exod.39:32,43; 40:33). The various objects of the cult correspond to the heavenly archetypes 'shown' by God to Moses 'on the mountain'. The Temple was not only a bit of the earth's topography, it was a bit of heaven on earth, set apart from mere earthly existence by its consecration. It was the point of connection between 'above' and 'below'. In this respect the Temple in Jerusalem was representative of the temple-experience of the whole ancient world. From the temple flowed all that established culture and divine order. The burning of the temple at Ephesus in the year 356 B.C. was a shock of an apocalyptic nature. Temple destruction let loose terror of the end of the world and foreboding of world catastrophes.

The end of the Temple in Jerusalem is a great rune indicating that everything which from the original divine revelation bound earthly existence to heavenly order will fall into dissolution. All that gave meaning and support to man on earth in the religion arising from his former connection with God will lose its power. In the twentieth century we see this development going on at an increasing pace. What happens thus over long periods of time is compressed in the prophetic pictures of human and cosmic catastrophes in the discourse on the Mount of Olives. It is a peculiarity of the visionary faculty that it can perceive whole series of events, stretching over long periods, in 'shortened perspective'. That these pictures should not be interpreted without qualification, as if the events they describe were imminent, is demonstrated by words like '*kairoi*', 'times of the Gentiles', the pagan peoples' destinies, which are still to be fulfilled between the fall of the Temple and the end of the world (Luke 21:24), or by the prophecy that the Gospel will be preached throughout the inhabited world before the end comes (Matt.24:14).

Christ's coming again is preceded by the appearance of 'the sign of the Son of man in heaven' (Matt.24:30). Heaven has become empty since sun and moon have lost their glory and the stars have fallen from heaven. Again one need not think of a single happening. Concentrated in this picture is the gradual de-spiritualization of man's outlook. In their shining, sun, moon and stars were once the appearances of cosmic spiritual powers. Paul still speaks about the individual glory of each star, which has its own '*doxa*', its special *aura* (1Cor.15:41). Devout contemplation of the stars once enabled man to become aware of the 'multitude of the heavenly host' and the spiritual hierarchies in their divine order. If one looks only materialistically into the starry worlds, the eye of the spirit being blind, then sun and moon lose their glory and the stars fall from heaven. Instead of what belongs to the past, instead of the original revelation carried through the ages from the time of creation, there now opens for a humanity deprived of its gods an entirely new approach to the divine. When 'most men's love' grows 'cold' (Matt.24:12)—the power of loving once naturally available to man, the cry of longing for 'humanity' rises up and then, out of deprivation, the word 'humanity' has a special significance. Thus a new awareness of the mystery of Man, incarnated in Christ Jesus, is being prepared. In the chapter, 'Knowledge of Man' we mentioned the fact that, so far, Christianity has hardly been aware of the profound connection of the '*humanum*', of what is essentially human, with the Being of Christ. This is revealed in the fact that the term Christ most frequently uses of Himself—Son of Man—has hardly been grasped by Christian theology. It can be taken quite literally: He who comes from divine realms enters into human existence to the point of human death, whence He rises in a new form as the new God bearing the stigmata, who was not in heaven before. He is at the same time the true 'Man', God's image, who has grown into the dimensions of Resurrection and Ascension. Peter, speaking of Christ's death (Acts 2:24), uses the word '*odino*', 'birth-throes'. What was then born out of death could proceed only from complete union with man's earthly existence, and thus is, in the true sense of the world, Son of Man. It is the future form of man, reaching far beyond all that was hitherto considered human, 'the joyful beginning of a more exalted humanity' as Novalis says. In the heavens which had become empty there now appears the 'sign', the 'rune' of the 'Son of Man' as a new and powerful ideal of the future. This stage, which still has something abstract about it, is followed by the real vision of Christ Himself appearing before the newly awakened spiritual insight of mankind. 'They will see the Son of man coming on the clouds of heaven with power (*dynamis*) and great glory (*doxa*—revealing light).' With Him come the angels. The consequence of 'becoming Christian' is a new awakening towards the spiritual realms of the hierarchies. 'He will send out his angels with a loud trumpet call, and they will gather his elect from the four winds' (Matt.24:31). Man's guidance by angels will be ever more noticeable, even in the way people meet each other 'by destiny'. Those belonging together in spirit will recognize one another from whatever corner of the earth they come and despite all that separated them in former times.

What was thus concentrated in the pictures of the Gospel expands into events reaching far into time and space. The idea of repeated lives on earth would not come into conflict with that, but, on the contrary, make it all really feasible through its actual historical realization.

The concentration of extensive series of events in one picture is also the key to Paul's apocalypse (1Thess.4:13–17). Paul pursues the question of the relationship of the departed souls to Christ's coming again. 'Through Jesus, God will bring with him those who have fallen asleep.' Those who have fallen 'asleep' from their earthly bodies have gained an existence full of life; God lets them walk in the other world in union with Christ, whose ways they share, with Him as their guide. Those who die in Christ also share in the second coming, even before those still living on earth, as in Goethe's *Faust* the mountain peaks '*früh des ewigen Lichts geniessen dürfen* (may enjoy the eternal light early)' which only later reaches the valleys. 'The Lord himself will descend from heaven with a cry of command' (4:16). With this cry (*keleusma*), something like a great command begins to resound through the spiritual world: 'The time has come'. 'The archangel's call' would lead one to think of Michael. In the spiritual outlook of Anthroposophy, Michael plays an important role. His mission is shown especially as the spiritualization of man's powers of thinking and willing on which so much depends today, but which are filled to a formidable extent by materialism. He would lead man's intelligence to the divine, and prepare mankind, truly 'come of age', for Christ.

The call of the archangel is followed by 'the sound of the trumpet of God', also mentioned in the Mount of Olives apocalypse (Matt.24:31)—'he will send out his angels with a loud trumpet call'. In the Apocalypse of John this motif unfolds to the sevenfold angelic blowing of trumpets. In the sound of the trumpet penetrating to the marrow of the bones, the awakening call of the spiritual world was experienced. In these three stages —the cry of command, the archangel's call, the sound of the trumpet of God—'the Lord himself will descend from heaven'.

We remarked in a previous chapter (see p. 33 ff.) that the word '*parousia*' indicates rather a 'being present' than a 'coming'. The Risen One, who said, 'I am with you always', is present. His 'coming' occurs in the field of human consciousness, which wakes up to this fact—the only way it can really 'come' to man. This principal insight, however, should be completed from another aspect. Through this awakening of man, Christ, though already present, also becomes active on His side. In the twenty-eighth chapter of Matthew's Gospel, for instance, it is reported how the Risen One sojourned with His disciples on the mountain but how not all of them, as far as their understanding was concerned, lived up to that experience. 'But some doubted' (Matt.28:17). Thereupon, in manifesting Himself, Christ did something further to meet their inadequate powers of perception. 'Jesus came' (28:18), and then He could *speak* to them. In a similar way, the Risen One, revealing Himself at the sea of Tiberias, 'moves' towards His disciples. John's narrative lets one see that there are various levels of supersensible awareness. The disciples beheld the figure on the beach but 'did not know that it was Jesus' (21:4). To the disciple whom Jesus loved recognition dawned first: 'It is the Lord' (21:7). Having come ashore, they had breakfast with the Risen One. 'Now none of the disciples dared to ask him, "Who are you?" They knew it was the Lord' (21:12). This is a strange hovering between not knowing and yet knowing. Friedrich Rittelmeyer once spoke of the dream-like quality of this wondrous scene. Then Jesus 'came' and took the bread (21:13). How did He 'come', since He was already together with the disciples for the meal at the charcoal fire? Again we have in this 'coming' a move on the part of the supersensible to increase insufficient human perception.—In this way, too, regarding His coming again, a dynamic activity of Christ is involved, *a movement towards man*. This means an addition to the more passive aspect that underlies the reading in Luke (17:30) where the day of His coming again is 'when the Son of man is revealed (*apokalyptetai*—uncovered)'. That He Himself contributes something to His revelation is clearly expressed by Paul with the words: 'For the Lord himself will descend from heaven' (1Thess.4:16).

This descent, however, does not take Him again into the lower regions of the *sarx*. He does not walk on the physical earth a second time; He graciously descends within the supersensible world, which itself has various levels. Paul was able to differentiate a first, second and third heaven out of his own supersensible experiences (2Cor.12:2). In the Buddhist story of Buddha's death, his movements up and down between different levels of the higher worlds are precisely described as a matter of course. Yet such truths are also not unknown in the New Testament. The Letter to the Hebrews speaks of Christ, the 'great high priest who has passed through the heavens' (4:14). Thus Christ at His coming again meets men, as it were, at the edge of the supersensible world, and consequently, for their part, they can now ascend to meet Him there. While descending through the spiritual spheres, Christ also passes through the region where those dwell who have died in the Lord—'And the dead in Christ will rise first; then we who are alive, who are left, shall be caught up together with them in the clouds to meet the Lord in the air; and so we shall always be with the Lord' (1Thess.4:16–17). The great movement starts in the region of the dead, just as in Holy Week the events of Saturday precede Easter morning. Even the world of the dead undergoes changes. What is so very concisely expressed in Paul's letter indicates a future phase in the relationship between the living and the dead, one in which a higher form of living together is no longer impeded by the separation through death—'we . . . together with them'. The mention of the clouds shows a connection with the Ascension. Then, those left behind on earth lost spiritual sight of the ascending Christ; He disappeared from them into the clouds. Now, however, not only do they see Him again revealing Himself out of the clouds, they themselves are lifted up into higher existence, to find themselves no longer 'left behind', but united with the dead. The 'air' to which men are taken up is the true symbol of the unrestricted new mode of existence which has overcome earth's gravity—there is a movement in the opposite direction to Adam's fall. The word '*harpazein*' used for the removal into airy regions indicates a not undramatic, and by no means gentle, process. Human souls who have desperately clung to material existence are torn from the deadly power of matter by the redeeming power of Christ.

According to the text in question, there is no doubt that Paul, when he wrote the First Letter to the Thessalonians, thought it possible that these eschatological events could happen during his lifetime. Through his experience at Damascus, Paul was also touched by the light of the future world of the Last Day and felt its breath upon him, and so was drawn into thinking of the 'end' as near. That does not mean that his Thessalonian apocalypse is invalid. The pictures he saw are in themselves true, only we have to translate them from the sphere of 'imaginations' into thoughts we can understand today. Anthroposophy shows us that such imagination does not mean an abstract idea expressed in a picture for pedagogical reasons, or anything in the way of mere dreams or irresponsible phantasies. Goethe felt his way towards true imagination when he spoke of an 'exact phantasy'. Imaginative consciousness in this sense does not invent, but finds its images as spontaneous phenomena. They must not be drawn on to the material level, which would result in absurd phantasies. They are like windows through which can be seen a supersensible reality that wishes to reveal itself. Through translation into the language of everyday consciousness errors might occur, as for Paul when he expected the realization of those visions in the immediate future. The course of history has meanwhile corrected the erroneous conclusions which could understandably come about in the early days of Christianity. Nevertheless, the great vision of the Thessalonian apocalypse remains valid, as well as what is said about the close community between departed souls and those 'left behind', and about the elimination of that separation known to those on earth as 'being left behind'. The unfolding necessary for a modern consciousness of the comprehensive content concentrated like a seed in the visionary language of eschatology involves a differentiation between Christ's 'coming again' and 'the Last Day'. In Paul's apocalypse, this distinction is not made. In the Mount of Olives apocalypse, 'resurrection' itself is not mentioned. In John's Apocalypse, the appearance of Christ in the clouds is already included in the fourteenth chapter (Rev.14:14), while the final conquest of death is first described considerably later, in the twentieth chapter (20:14). In between, in the nineteenth chapter, there is the appearance of Christ as the 'white rider'. In Luke's Gospel an important indication is given. Just as we thank the evangelist Luke for keeping the sentence about the 'times (*kairoi*) of the Gentiles', which has preserved the more extensive time scale of the Mount of Olives apocalypse, so he is also the only New Testament author who has handed down to us the sentence about 'the [apparently several] days of the Son of man'. 'The days are coming when you will desire to see one of the days of the Son of man' (17:22).

Otherwise, also with Luke, the 'day of the Son of man' is a definite expression for the actual time of the 'coming again', as in the passage already quoted (17:30): '*the* day when the Son of man is revealed (*apokalyptetai*)'. Nevertheless, verse 22 says: 'one of the days of the Son of man'. Is the 'coming again' something that happens several times? At His first coming, Christ entered the world of *sarx*. He had to accept a material body in order to 'reach the sight of' human beings (to use a Rilkean expression), who were no longer able to behold the spiritual world. In this visible body He went through the death on Golgotha. With the Ascension, He took on a mode of existence which for the time being was not accessible to earthly man. His coming again 'in the same way as you saw Him go into heaven' implies a progress in man's consciousness. Returning, He does not again walk earthly ground, but He becomes visible in His supersensible form. Like Paul once at Damascus, mankind will come to its own direct experience that Christ is actually spiritually there in person. A second 'meeting' of mankind with Christ occurs, but this time on a higher level. That it is possible this time to meet Him in the supersensible is already a result of His redeeming deed on His first coming in the flesh. The word to 'meet' occurs in the parable of the Wise and Foolish Maidens (Matt.25:6) and in Paul's Thessalonian apocalypse (1Thess.4:17). Since, according to Paul's account, Christ 'descends' at His coming again, but without touching the earth, it can be imagined that Christ, as we have already said, meets man at the lower edge of the spiritual world, so that His coming does not happen in the highest but the lowest of the heavens. This would be 'one' day of the Son of Man. Anthroposophy speaks of a coming of Christ in the 'etheric' realm. This region of life-giving and formative forces is the lowest level of the super-sensible world which reaches nearest to man. It is intended that man should become ever more aware of this realm and therein meet the living Christ face to face. In a distant future, according to the increasing supersensible faculties of man, a meeting is designed on an even higher level, that spiritual realm where what is soul-like, the 'astral' dwells. And finally, in an even more distant future, and again on a higher level, comes a meeting of the true human ego, then fully awakened, with the Ego of Christ. Thus the unique reading in Luke about several days of the Son of man could be filled with real life.—At any rate, this sentence of Luke gives an important indication of a much greater dimension of time for the eschatological visions of the New Testament than one might suppose from the first erroneous and literal interpretation of them.

With this broader outlook, reincarnation becomes increasingly obvious since thereby men pass through the great evolutionary phases and are allowed to share ever more conscious and intimate meetings with the Christ.

The most explicit eschatology is contained in the Apocalypse of John.

Human Evolution in the Apocalypse of John

We shall now survey the Apocalypse in an endeavour to see what it has to say concerning *mankind's Christian progress*. This continually changes the scene of its realization between *earth* and *heaven*. Christianity—on the one side embodied on earth, on the other existing in heaven—increasingly develops into an important factor working in the eschatological drama. At the end, upper and lower world penetrate each other. A 'new earth', made new by what has come from above, joins a 'new heaven', which itself has been rejuvenated by what happened through Christ on earth. Out of this merging of the two there comes the New Jerusalem, which is both 'heaven' and 'earth'. The Christ-Mystery, unifying heaven and earth, has become powerful within a Christendom now ripe for it. John's Apocalypse shows in the sequence of its visions this process of ripening. From that survey we shall return once more to reincarnation.

*

The Risen One appears to John on Patmos and gives him the messages to the seven churches. In these seven churches is displayed the spectrum of Christianity as it exists on *earth* with various nuances of striving and suffering, of failures and achievements, each with its characteristic differences of purpose. The great and final goals, up to the ascension-experience and sitting on the throne (3:21), already shine out in the promises to the churches. 'He who conquers, I will grant him to sit with me on my throne, as I myself conquered and sat down with my Father on his throne'. This last image of the 'throne' opens the great vision of Chapters 4 and 5, in the midst of which stands the divine throne. John is drawn into the upper world: 'Come up hither' (4:1). He becomes a witness of the eternal '*Sanctus*' resounding there, and the new element that comes into the eternal world through the Deed of Golgotha. The Lamb of sacrifice brings His own deed before the Father's throne. This is echoed in the 'New Song' which the exalted beings of the innermost circle utter and which is added to the eternal '*Sanctus*'. There are the four cherubim 'living creatures' and the twenty-four elders who, in adoration of what has been made known, give voice to the New Song which then continues through wider concentric circles of angelic hosts and elemental creatures praising God. The New Song, issuing from the innermost circle round the throne, contains an ingredient which comes from men on earth, in whose midst the sacrifice of the Lamb took place: 'the prayers of the saints' (5:8). Men living on earth devoted to Christ are not yet able to join in that song, but impulses break forth from their souls that can be received in the heavens and become visible as the smoke of incense, which rises up from the golden bowls of the elders, together with the New Song.

★

The 'prayers of the saints' rise up from Christians living on earth. After the opening of the seals has begun, Christians who have gone through martyrdom now themselves appear in the *upper world*. The seer sees them under the heavenly altar (6:9). It is remarkable that the word '*psychai*' is used for them, souls who, even in a disembodied state, have an independent conscious existence after death. It is the first time that Christian souls are recognized by John in that realm. In comparison with what will be said later about them in the course of the Apocalypse, a certain hesitancy and reluctance still overlies this first mention. They are not yet fully satisfied with their new form of existence, which is expressed in the question which arises from their souls 'with a loud voice'. 'How long . . . ?' This question is rendered by John in words reminiscent of the Old Testament. It can indeed often be noticed in the Apocalypse that John, with a certain piety, is attentive to the connection with earlier apocalyptic 'schools' and occasionally uses ancient sacred forms of expression into which, however, he pours the new Christian content. 'How long before thou wilt judge and avenge our blood on those who dwell upon the earth?' (6:10). 'Avenge'—'*ek-dikein*', for the sake of justice to let the consequences follow according to the law of sowing and reaping. The law of sowing and reaping, of deed and consequence, is also valid in the case of Christ's death. According to its special conditions, however, this death has redeeming consequences. Through their sacrifice, the Christian martyrs are helping to give reality to something of the redeeming power of Christ's death. What in the formulations of the Old Testament sounds like a cry for vengeance, in the Christian sense is really the question about the meaning of the fruit of sacrifice. The sufferings of the martyrs seem to disappear in the world—is there no fruitful result to be seen?

The divine answer to the question, 'How long?' indicates 'Not yet'. They are told 'to rest a little longer until the number of their fellow servants and their brethren should be complete, who were to be killed as they themselves had been'. If it is to bring forth its full fruit, the unique Deed of Golgotha needs a response from mankind. Providence has so arranged that the redeeming deed, which could not be fulfilled by man himself, but only through grace by a divine being, does not mean mere passivity for those redeemed. In economic policy, where there is a question of giving help, the concept of 'constructive aid' has arisen, whereby those to be helped should not be tempted to become lazy, but through the way aid is given be encouraged to contribute to it from their own activity. Christ's deed of redemption is in the highest sense 'constructive aid'. Paul could boldly say: 'I complete what is lacking in Christ's afflictions for the sake of his body, that is, the church' (Col.1:24). If he inwardly accepts the redeeming deed, man cannot help at the same time actively joining in its fulfilment so that Christ's sacrifice is brought to life anew in him. The questioning martyrs are referred to the fact that the response man should give to Golgotha has not yet been realised to the extent deemed sufficient by Providence. The divine 'economy' counts on a still greater contribution of sacrifice from mankind towards the fruitful completion of Christ's sacrifice. So the souls of the martyrs find themselves integrated into a more far-reaching divine purpose. Meanwhile they should 'rest a little longer'. They are allowed for a time to let the terrible experiences they had on earth lessen their impact and die away, and to take a deep breath in the calm of the divine world. The answer they are given is connected with a further development of their existence after death as a result of their martyrdom. 'Then they were each given a white robe' (6:11). While they let the horrors of their suffering fade away, and free themselves of the painful questions in the calm of the spiritual world, the excarnated souls are given a supersensible covering, instead of their earthly bodies they no longer need, a new 'organ' with which they are 'further clothed' (2Cor.5:4). The loss below corresponds to a gain above; they become more active and responsible citizens of the higher world, being granted such a fine, light-woven organism, though it is one not yet identical with the resurrection body.

★

In the pause between the sixth and seventh seals, the 144,000 are 'sealed'. We are again looking at the *earthly* scene. The number, of course, is not an arithmetically arrived-at figure. It is 'heard' in the spirit (7:4) as a divine figure ringing out, imposing order. Only the sum total of all the nuances of 'being man' possible under the stars results in the great 'Man of all men', the symphony of the whole human race. Instead of the people of the Old Testament ordered in twelve groups according to the stars, Christians appear as God's people. They stand on earth in the catastrophic and apocalyptic storms which began with the opening of the seals. But the sealing of the 144,000 happens in a moment of calm. Providence allows such moments of profound, divine calm in the midst of disasters following each other in swift succession. In this calm, John sees an angel ascending from the rising of the sun, an Easter angel as it were, who seals the 144,000 on their foreheads with the seal of the living God. Christianity on earth has proceeded so far that the Being of Christ can be imprinted right into the body as a '*character indelebilis*'.

The sealing marks a stage of development towards the resurrection body. In what He says about 'the bread of life', in the sixth chapter of John's Gospel, Christ applies the picture of the sealing to Himself. He will not offer food that perishes but food which endures to eternal life, 'for on him has God the Father set his seal' (6:27). The feeding with the food for eternity still belongs, then, to the future—'which the Son of man will give to you' *after* the fulfilment of the Mystery of Golgotha, which shines out prophetically in this Passover at the Sea of Galilee. But a year later Christ will overcome death and be able to give man the food that builds up the resurrection body, because He bears the spiritual imprint of the 'sealing' right in His body. The vision of the apocalyptist shows how the sealing begins to work on those devoted to Christ, as a preparation for the resurrection on the Last Day.

*

The sealing of Christians living on earth is followed by a vision which once again shows Christians in the *other world* as 'a great multitude which no man could number, from every nation, from all tribes and peoples and tongues' (7:9). Though this vision immediately follows the previous one, the seer notices that the two pictures refer to different times. 'After this (*meta tauta*) I looked' (7:9). This '*tauta*' is plural. The chapter also begins with 'After this . . .' but there it is the singular in Greek—'*meta touto*'. 'The expression "*meta tauto*" indicates greater intervals of time.'* Between the two visions a great deal may have happened behind the scenes concerning 'the great tribulation' referred to in verse fourteen. Perhaps Christians sealed during their earth existence have meanwhile suffered death and experienced the ascent into the other world. The impression of the 'multitude which no man could number' makes it clear once more that the 144,000 is not used as an arithmetical figure.

In comparison with the first vision of martyrs the change is obvious. The white robe is not this time given in the course of after-death experiences, but those appearing now have already in their life as Christians on earth, through their devotion to Christ, 'washed' the finer sheaths of their nature, 'made them white (*leukainein*) in the blood of the Lamb' (7:14). Already on earth they have cleansed their 'aura' and, through the power of Christ's blood, formed the fine organism of light which appears after death in the higher world. They stand 'with palm branches in their hands' and, instead of tormentedly questioning 'How long?', they sing the great solemn hymn: 'Salvation (*soteria*) to our God . . . and to the Lamb' (7:10 literally). The dative—'*to* our God'—is important. The deliverance of the world has come from God; sending Christ, the Father has said as it were: 'Salvation to man'. The '*soteria*', the great salvation, has really reached the earth, has 'come' to men. Now it radiates from truly Christian souls as thanks returned from the lower to the upper regions of God's creation. Christians who have died bring something of importance to the upper world. From men, the song of praise is taken up by angels, who through men gain contact with the redeeming deed which was not fulfilled in heaven but on earth (compare 1Pet.1:12).

The dead are privileged to become active in the upper world. They 'serve him day and night within his temple' (7:15). Another different picture is then added to this aspect: they walk in the upper world on paths where the Lamb 'will guide them to springs of living water' (7:17). As in the ancient world Hermes was the Psychopompos, the guide of souls after death, so here

* Christoph Rau, *Struktur und Rhythmus im Johannesevangelium*, Verlag Urachhaus, Stuttgart, 1972, p. 47.

it is Christ who leads them in their development, whereby, as if on a kind of mountain ascent, they come nearer to the places of life's origin. 'Guide'—in Greek '*hodegein*', which means, literally, 'to guide on paths'. Now the inner reconcilliation with the terrible things they endured on earth can come about—expressed in the wonderfully simple and tender picture of God wiping away the tears from their eyes.

Immediately following this we are again reminded of the Christians living *on earth*. Once again, the ascending *prayers of the saints* become noticeable in heaven. The angels accept these devout feelings striving upwards, they do something to them, they intersperse them as it were with additional substance—'much incense to mingle with the prayers of all the saints' (8:3). What rises up from below calls forth an answer from above; fire from the heavenly altar can be thrown on the earth (8:5).

The progressively destructive catastrophes that break out as the trumpets resound afflict the earthly world and mankind itself ever more severely. Before the seventh trumpet sounds the seer is asked to measure with a measuring rod 'the temple of God and the altar and those who worship there' (11:1). The court outside the temple is abandoned, the holy city trampled by the heathen. We are *on earth*. It is not the heavenly temple and altar that are meant. It is not even just Jerusalem, though the destruction of Jerusalem might have provided the picture of the holy city 'trampled over'.

One could apply the sentence, 'it will be and is already now' here, too. At the end of the Apocalypse the holy city will descend from heaven as the heavenly Jerusalem, spontaneously, it seems, without any sort of preparations. And yet they are there throughout the Apocalypse. What was once 'holy city' in the ancient world, however, is irretrievably lost to the profane. But in the midst of the destruction of the values of the past there springs up through Christ's deed in the human realm on earth a new and transformed world. In the Middle Ages the seekers of the Holy Grail did not search for a geographically located castle, but for that invisibly growing 'Easter' kingdom on earth. Thus John sees in the midst of the annihilation the 'temple' with the 'altar'. It is evident that it is not a question of material measurements since he also has to measure 'those who worship there' with the reed given to him, though it is not yet the 'measuring rod of gold' with which he must later measure the New Jerusalem (21:15). On the way to the final goal this is, as it were, an interim assessment to find out how far the growing future has already developed.

In connection with this, the 'two witnesses' appear. They are clearly characterized as Moses and Elijah *reincarnated* on earth. They are clothed in sackcloth (11:3). The representatives of the divine world appear in the midst of the catastrophes, outwardly inconspicuous, but work with extraordinary spiritual power until they succumb to the 'beast that ascends from the bottomless pit'. This, as it is explicitly said, will 'conquer them' (11:7). Real development does not proceed in an unbroken direct line forward as naïve optimism may imagine. It is a movement which through ever recurring obstacles, reverses and backslidings nevertheless gradually achieves its aim. In all spiritual development just such negative factors are significant for their deepening effect. The word 'conquer' is one of the basic words of the Apocalypse. Each of the seven letters ends with a promise to the one who 'conquers', who 'overcomes'. Man can reach his goal only if he consciously overcomes the very real negative possibilities that exist for his development; this is obviously connected with the mystery of freedom. On the way to this 'conquest', the inner path also leads through experiences of 'being conquered'. In just this way man matures for the final victory. The two witnesses are conquered and killed in 'the great city which is allegorically called Sodom and Egypt, where their Lord was crucified' (11:8). As the heavenly Jerusalem has its preparatory stages, so, too, has the fallen Babylon, the embodiment of that part of mankind which has lost the relationship to the higher world and, moreover, wants it lost. In that great city with its purely materialistic, god-forsaken civilization, the Christ is, as it were, permanently crucified. But the death of the two witnesses is followed by an Easter and Ascension-like event. A resurrection in the body occurs, followed by an ascent to heaven 'in a cloud' (11:12). It is explicitly said that both happen 'in the sight' of their foes. Christ's Resurrection and Ascension were actual events in the world, but visible only to the eyes of those who were inwardly prepared for it. Nothing was seen by Caiaphas and Pilate. The eleventh chapter of the Apocalypse points to a future when the reality of the supersensible will more and more forcefully claim man's attention and even make itself apparent to those who do not want to know anything about it. In the Apocalypse two different words are used for 'seeing' to indicate that this resurrection and ascension is not a question of a crude material process. Men 'see' the corpses of the two witnesses; here the word '*blepein*' is used (11:9). It is normal seeing, while at the resurrection (11:11) and once more at the ascension (11:12) '*theorein*' is used of their awareness, which has a stronger spiritual connotation. As on Easter morning, here, too, comes the great earthquake. The earth vibrates in sympathy when a body which is closely connected with it undergoes such a metamorphosis.

Here it is not only a question of departed souls becoming active in the upper world, but of something that lies on the way between the Resurrection at Easter and the Last Day, something, to put it cautiously, of a resurrection and ascension nature. Here, too, there are preparatory stages. One such in the past, before Golgotha, that came about through the still remaining original paradisal forces, has been seen in the mysteriously taciturn passage in Genesis (5:24) which says of Enoch, the seventh patriarch after Adam, that he walked with God, was taken up by him and was no more on the earth. In the light of this prophetic dawn, perhaps we might even find dimly understandable the strange account by Matthew in connection with Good Friday and Easter that 'many bodies of the saints who had fallen asleep were raised, and coming out of the tombs after his resurrection they went into the holy city and appeared to many' (27:52–53). Though according to Paul the actual resurrection body is to come into existence on the Last Day in one brief moment, it is nevertheless only the final stage in a long development. Already the pre-Christian 'saints' had begun the first stages of gradually spiritually changing not only the finer elements of their own natures but also the earth itself. Without Christ's deed, this transformation begun already before His time would have remained incomplete. Through it, however, these initial resurrection-like occurrences were so to speak confirmed and substantiated. The going of the risen saints into the holy city, as Jerusalem is called in only one other place in the Gospel (Matt.4:5), might even indicate the secret that with each spiritualization of an earthly body the dynamic realm of the New Jerusalem is already touched upon.

The long lack of association of Christian theology with real spirituality has resulted in much too rigidly conceptualized thinking and too hastily arrived at conclusions. If the resurrection body of man is to appear fully only on the Last Day, that should not exclude the idea that there may be earlier events which are not identical with the final achievement, but lie on the way to it.

★

After the sounding of the seventh trumpet, exactly in the middle of the book, the name of Michael is mentioned (12:7). 'The war in heaven' between Michael and his angels on the one side and the dragon and his angels on the other ends with the dragon being thrown to the earth. This war happens in *supersensible* realms. There is no mention of men, either incarnated or excarnated, in this pictorial description. Only in the great hymn of victory, which the seer heard through powerful Inspiration (12:10), is the mystery revealed that even in this supersensible event man was a contributory and even a most important factor. The hymn begins with the words: 'Now the salvation and the power and the kingdom of our God and the authority (*exousia*) of his Christ have come'. Thereby the hymn of the departed souls is taken up again: 'Salvation to our God . . . and to the Lamb' (7:10 literally). The word 'salvation'—'*soteria*', the great deliverance—is not used in the Apocalypse anywhere else except a third time at the end (19:1). If one looks at the Apocalypse as a whole, which is essential for a proper understanding of it, it is evident that these three passages where *soteria* is mentioned together form a pattern. In 7:10 we noticed the significant dative—*to* our God, *to* the Lamb—which means that *soteria* once received by man now streams back from man to God as an offering, a great thanksgiving. In 12:10 it is not the dative but the genitive which is used: the salvation *of* our God. The offering has reached the higher world and now belongs to it. It is wrong to think man has nothing to give to God and argue that since everything anyway belongs to God the thought of offering would be a primitive error. Certainly in its origin everything is God's. But, in order to let man develop in the freedom intended for him, 'in his own image', God granted him a sphere of freedom. As the Psalm already said: 'The heavens are the LORD's heavens, but the earth he has given to the sons of men' (115:16). 'My son, give me your heart' (Prov. 23:26): thus the religious could also hear God speaking to men. Man can also, however, withhold his heart from God. In the emancipation of his earthly existence he has the possibility of alienating God's property. Knowing the facts, however, he may make the effort to return the alienated property to God as a freely made offering. It is not impious arrogance for man to say that he has something to give to God. It has been thus arranged by God out of His love of our growing freedom. It is in connection with Christ's sacrifice coming to life in man that Christians make their offering to God. The three *soteria* passages represent three phases: in 7:10 there is the offering (dative); in 12:10 the arrival of that offering at a great moment of world events ('now'—'*arti*'), while in 19:1 the *soteria* has not only just 'now' come (as in 12:10—'*egeneto*'), but it *is* God's, quite clearly existing and resting in Him. We can put the three *soteria* passages next to each other:

7:10 *Soteria* to our God who sits upon the throne, and to the Lamb!

12:10 Now the *soteria* and the power and the kingdom of our God and the authority of his Christ have come.

19:1 Hallelujah! *Soteria* and glory and power belong to our God.

The first passage precedes the opening of the seventh (last) seal. The second follows the sounding of the seventh (last) trumpet. The third comes after the pouring out of the seventh (last) bowl of the wrath of God. Important moments in the Apocalyptic progression through seals, trumpets, bowls of wrath are marked by these three passages.

That the salvation and the power finally 'belong to God' is connected with men becoming Christian on earth. Already after the seventh trumpet the song of praise becomes audible: 'We give thanks to thee, Lord God Almighty, . . . that thou hast taken thy great power and begun to reign' (11:17). This, however, establishes at least a period of decreased power of the Almighty, right down to the powerlessness of the Deity on earth, resulting in the Passion. God 'everything to every one'

(1Cor.15:28) is not a description of a present situation but a preview of a fulfilment to come when, through what is offered from the earth, the Deity resumes His true omnipotence. This is already foreshadowed in the motif in the Psalms: 'The LORD reigns' (93:1; 97:1; 99:1. Also 47:2'. . . the LORD . . . a great king over all the earth.') And how, in the Lord's Prayer, could one pray for the coming of His kingdom and the fulfilment of His will on earth if that were already accomplished and self-evident?

The word 'now' (*arti*) with which the hymn of the Michael chapter begins is rarely, but emphatically, used in the New Testament.*

That Michael's battle has been won *not without man* becomes evident in the words: 'And they have conquered him [the dragon] by the blood of the Lamb and by the word of their testimony, for they loved not their lives (*psyche*) even unto death' (12:11). This is a classical example of how the visions of the seer often one-sidedly include only *one* aspect and are open to completion. According to the vision, Michael with his angels achieved the victory. The hymn, for its part also one-sided, can express the facts of the case with the words: '*They* have conquered him. They, who in the hymn are also called 'our brethren', which indicates that those who sing the hymn with 'a loud voice in heaven' are Christian souls living in the

* In the Gospel of Matthew, which frequently, like John's, has a mysterious use of numbers, the word occurs seven times (3:15; 9:18; 11:12; 23:39; 26:29,53,64). Three times '*ap' arti*', 'from now on', marks Christ's sacrifice as the decisive moment, the turning point of world history. This is at the end of His public ministry, at the beginning of Holy Week (23:39—R.S.V. 'again'), at the Last Supper (26:29—R.S.V. 'again'), and at the great solemn confession before the High Priest and the council (26:64—R.S.V. 'hereafter').—Also in John's Gospel it is one of the important words whose appearance in the text is owing to a divine numerical order. Seven times '*arti*' is used to underline the actual moment in time: at the healing of the Man Born Blind (9:19,25—R.S.V. 'now'), at the Washing of the Disciples' Feet (13:7,33,37—R.S.V. 'now'), in the Farewell Discourses (16:12,31—R.S.V. 'now'). Three times 'until now' (*eos arti*): at Cana the good wine was kept 'until now' (John 2:10), 'My Father is working still' (John 5:17)—'Hitherto you have asked nothing in my name' (16:24). Three times 'from now on' (*ap' arti*): '[From now on] you will see heaven opened' (1:51 R.S.V. omits this phrase), 'I tell you this now, before it takes place' (13:19), 'henceforth you know him [the Father]' (14:7). It is a word which emphasises the uniqueness of Christ's deeds and can also consequently be used for those moments in the further development of Christianity where this fundamental 'now' flashes up anew. So it comes as the first word in the Michael hymn in which the '*arti*' clearly resounds in its apocalyptic quality.

other world. Both aspects are right. It is Michael with his angels: and it is man, who can be the sword of Michael on earth—through 'the blood of the Lamb'.

⋆

With the throwing down of the dragon, the view is again *towards the earth*. The woman who appears in heaven as mankind's cosmic soul, adorned with sun and moon and stars, now gains a bare living in the 'wilderness', and 'the rest of her offspring', as Christians are here called in this significant and mystical expression, are exposed on earth to the attacks of the dragon (12:17). It is one of the revealing paradoxes of the Apocalypse that the heavenly jubilation at the victory—as if it had not rung out—is followed by the triumph of the Antichrist on earth. The victory has been decided above, but it still takes a while till it comes into effect below; the phases are not simultaneous. The beast from the bottomless pit (11:7) conquered the two witnesses, and this event is now being repeated. The beast 'was allowed to make war on the saints and to conquer them' (13:7). The beast 'was allowed' just as Pilate was 'given' power 'from above' over the life and death of Jesus (John 19:11). The experience of defending a hopeless position also belongs to the process of Christian development towards maturity. It is endurance, patience (*hypomoné*) that enables the saints on earth to survive the regime of the Antichrist, which rises to a terrible system of compulsion so that 'no one can buy or sell unless he has the mark, that is, the name of the beast' (in contrast to God's seal) 'on the right hand or the forehead' (13:17,16). The patience of the saints and their confident faith despite everything stand like an erratic boulder in the midst of the world ruled by the Antichrist.

The saints, patient and faithful, at the same time know that they share in a higher level of existence. As John beheld the temple in the great city and those praying there as a kind of non-geographical region of the Holy Grail, so Christians living in the realm of the Antichrist find each other united in spirit in a higher region where they are lifted beyond the activities of the beast—this is the Mount Zion which is also part of the still growing heavenly Jerusalem. On this holy mountain John sees Christ in the form of the Lamb in the midst of the 144,000. The

Letter to the Hebrews also mentions Mount Zion as the spiritual meeting place of Christians (12:22).

While the Antichrist does his evil work, those gathered around Christ receive a new higher faculty. Out of a sound from heaven, at first like the noise of rushing water and thunder, there arises a wonderful music of harps. The harp players sing the New Song (14:3).* It was first of all sung by the exalted beings of the innermost circle around the throne of God, the four cherubim, 'living beings' and the twenty-four elders, who also had harps in their hands. Man's contribution appeared only in the incense of the rising 'prayers of the saints'. Now the situation is different. The New Song which began in the innermost circle round the throne has spread in widening concentric circles. This time the harpers and singers are not the exalted beings of the innermost circle, but others who now play and sing 'to' them. Who these others are to whom the song has been handed over is not directly said. They let the song ring out to the 144,000 who, alone amongst men on earth, are those ready to hear this heavenly music, not only to hear, but even to 'learn' the New Song. While in the realm of Antichrist all man's deeper feelings are threatened with extinction, there dawns in the souls of the saints a whole new realm of feeling as a result of Christ's sacrifice. In the ancient cultures, the 'Old Song' still sounded from the creation, from the primal revelation. What existed as ancient culture is destroyed and this is connected with the 'trampling' of the holy city which is no longer a sanctuary. In Babylon all music has died (18:22). The New Song is a new music blossoming from souls permeated by Christ, a new realm of feeling, a new culture. But it does not come about by itself in the more dreamlike way of the Old Song for still immature souls; a mustering of inner forces is now needed, a holy *learning*—learning that entails the striving of one's ego to work consciously for the deepening of the inner life. In the Saviour's call, 'Come to me, all . . .' Christ says: 'Learn from me' (Matt.11:28,29). The 144,000 are 'virgins' in soul, and in spirit 'spotless' and without the deadly marks of falsehood. By virtue of the sealing in which they shared earlier, the 144,000 have become able to keep themselves free of the

* cf. Emil Bock, *The Apocalypse of St. John*, The Christian Community Press, London, 1957, 'Trumpets and Harps'.

imprint, the '*charagma*' of the beast. (This '*charagma*' appears seven times: 13:16,17; 14:9,11; 16:2; 19:20; 20:4). The seal on their foreheads is now being transformed into the inscription of the Lamb and the Father God (14:1). In a first foreshadowing of the distant goal in the sixth letter, to Philadelphia, the promise is given: 'I will write on him the name of my God, and the name of the city of my God, the new Jerusalem which comes down from my God out of heaven, and my own new name' (3:12).

This threefold naming changes to a twofold one in 14:1, till finally, on the completion of the heavenly Jerusalem, combining into the *one* divine name that unites God and the Lamb (22:4). It is a process in which the trinity first unfolds and then reunites. In 14:1 the aspect of the sacrifice of the Lamb is dominant.

In 14:12, for the seventh and last time, there is a reference to 'endurance' (*hypomoné*) which is now near its reward.

★

After the series of seven references to endurance or patience (1:9; 2:2,3,19; 3:10; 13:10; 14:12) has come to an end, its place is taken by another even more forceful apocalyptic series of seven: the Beatitudes (1:3; 14:13; 16:15; 19:9; 20:6; 22:7,14), which from now on follow each other more closely. In 14:13 there is the blessing of 'the dead who die in the Lord'. As in the Michael hymn (12:10) here again there also appears the distinctive 'now' (*arti*)—from now on, 'henceforth'. Here a question might arise. Has not the blessedness of the martyrs already been sung in a manner not to be surpassed in Chapter 7? Why now 'henceforth'? Again, one may well not find an answer by means of the analytical-logical approach familiar to us. Apocalyptic consciousness experiences the time element differently. The previous 'now' at the beginning of the Michael hymn (12:10) was, as the Antichrist chapter (13) goes on to show, in 'anticipation'—'above', the victory is already assured. The second 'now'—'henceforth' in 14:13—is, by comparison, in 'retrospect'. Though it was already true, only now does one become fully aware of the final triumph. The martyrs mentioned before had also 'died in the Lord'. After the sound of the seventh trumpet, however, what was already valid before appears once more in a new light, on the analogy of the experience that something learned long ago suddenly appears as a new discovery.

The word 'rest' ('they may rest from their labours') does not mean 'rest in the grave', any more than it does at the first appearance of the martyrs (6:11), but a deep inbreathing in the spirit. Indeed, the Apocalypse again and again shows that the dead are not idle. What they are resting from are the 'labours', the pain inseparable from all work on earth. After the Fall, Adam and Eve were not 'condemned to work'—they were busy before, cultivating and tending the garden. What makes working 'a curse' is the labour connected with 'thorns and thistles'. From this negative impact of earthly labour the blessed are released for a work that can proceed in restful harmony. Their 'rest' is not disturbed by their deeds 'which follow them'. Man's earthly deeds do not consist only as it were of a body; as they are being performed they are given a soul by particular feelings, and in spirit they carry particular intentions. A good deed done with egotistical intent would not be good because, although perhaps outwardly pleasing, it would in fact be despicable from the lack of honest intent. Human deeds are supersensible *beings* which follow close behind the doers and after death make themselves felt most forcefully. The deeds of those spoken of as 'blessed' in 14:13 do not cause disquiet in the life after death but rather bear that in them whereby the liberating inbreathing in the calm of the spirit can be experienced—'*for* their deeds follow them'. The beatitude of the dead leads to the coming of the Son of Man on the white cloud, which in the Apocalypse, as already mentioned, does not coincide with the final fulfilment.

The motif of the New Song occurs, slightly changed, for the third and last time in chapter 15, where preparation is made for the pouring out of the bowls of wrath, which has to precede the final fulfilment. Again a progression is observable. In 5:8 the highest beings of the innermost circle sing the song for the first time. In 14:2 its waves have already spread and sound forth to the 144,000 who have risen on Mount Zion and 'learn' the song. Quite clearly there now appear as harp players and singers those Christians who have conquered 'out of' the beast (so literally 15:2) and through their victory have freed themselves from his power and the might of his mark. They stand beside the sea of glass whose originally pure crystal now appears mingled with 'fire'—a higher union of crystal-clear purity and the burning fire of love to which the world's first form of creation has now advanced. The crystal sea is seen for the first time in the great vision of the throne in the fourth chapter (4:6). Those who have conquered play the 'harps of God'. David once soothed the demonic Saul with his harp playing. The New Song now receives a different name: 'the song of Moses' and 'the song of the Lamb' (15:3). In traditional apocalyptic scholarship, the great deliverance at the Red Sea after the exodus from the plague-ridden darkness of Egypt was the prototype of eschatological events. The exodus from Egypt happened under the sign of the sacrificial Passover Lamb. The exodus from the decaying world under the sway of the beast becomes possible through the sacrifice of the true Passover Lamb.

★

In the description of how the victors have won 'out of' the thraldom of the beast there is indicated—as well as in the Song of Moses—the great 'exodus' still to come, which has its prelude in all the foregoing exodus stories. In the parable of the Weeds and the Wheat both are allowed to grow together until the moment of harvest has come, and with it the separation of one from the other. Christians on earth have to suffer the régime of the beast in patience. Men opposed to the divine harden themselves more and more (16:9,11,21). The harlot Babylon is 'drunk with the blood of the saints' (17:6). In the unchristianized world—which appeared as 'the great city . . . Sodom and Egypt' and finally as Babylon falling into the abyss presents the counter picture to the heavenly Jerusalem—'was found the blood of prophets and of saints, and of all who have been slain on earth' (18:24). The call ringing out from heaven: 'Come out of her, my people (*laos*)' (18:4) means the final exodus. Thereafter comes the catastrophe of the 'great city', which according to 16:19 had already had its earlier stages.

★

The Babylon chapter (18) is followed by the vision of the white rider and his hosts. Here Christ is called by His most exalted name—'The Word of God'. 'And the armies of heaven, arrayed in fine linen, white and pure, followed him on white horses' (19:14). Who are those warriors who follow the Logos? This is quite clearly answered in an earlier passage. After the name 'Armageddon' has already prophetically occurred as the place of the decisive battle in 16:16, 17:14 contains a preview of the battle itself. The adversaries 'will make war on the Lamb, and the Lamb will conquer them, for he is Lord of lords and King of kings, *and those with him are called and chosen and faithful*'. Here appears the same title as in 19:16: 'Lord of lords' and 'King of kings'. This title might have been used by the great kings of the orient, yet, here again, as so often, previously coined phrases are taken over into the Apocalypse, but imbued with an entirely new meaning. In this context the title does not mean a mighty potentate. Here it should be taken literally: 'Lord of lords'. Christ cannot reveal His true being and working by commanding slaves and hangers-on, but only if men who are responsibly aware of their true being, who have called up lordly power and self-mastery from within themselves, join Him out of free will. John's prologue says that Christ 'came to his own' (*idioi*) who, for the very reason of their awakened ego-power should have been 'his own', yet, debasing this power into mere egotism, 'received him not' (John 1:11). This rejection, however, was not total. 'But to all who received him . . .' Those who received Christ in their innermost being as the great selfless Ego are truly 'his own'. They are not what is usually meant by 'lords', but they have placed the inner lordly power of their ego in the service of Christ. He is—to use Novalis's phrase—'the Ego of egos'. In regard to the white rider, the order of words is reversed, beginning with the kingly power: 'King of kings and Lord of lords' (19:16). In 17:14 the warriors of Christ are characterized in three ways: 'called and chosen and faithful'. 'Called and chosen' reminds us of the end of the parable of the royal Marriage Feast (Matt.22:14). Here, too, the words are used in connection with a 'marriage'. The chapter concerning the white rider is introduced by the proclamation of the 'marriage of the Lamb' (19:7). The heavenly Bridegroom joins Himself to mankind on earth. The union is expressed in the picture of a marriage and a meal. 'Blessed are those who are invited to the marriage supper of the Lamb' (19:9). The Bride's gown is described as 'fine linen, bright (*lampros*) and pure', a degree still brighter than the white (*leukos*) robe mentioned before. The adjective '*lampros*', radiantly bright, is also used for the crystal river of the water of life in the heavenly Jerusalem (22:1) and for the brightness of the morning star (22:16)—as well as already before in the description of the angels with the seven plagues who come out of the temple 'robed in pure bright linen' (15:6). Christ's armies are 'arrayed in fine linen, white and pure' (19:14). The word '*byssinos*' here used for linen has not so far been used for the white robes of blessed souls. It means an especially fine linen. This is again an enhancement, and it is the same word used shortly before for the marriage robe of the Bride of the Lamb (19:8).

According to the preview of 17:14 these warriors are not angels but human beings, Christians, who also have their share in the origin of the white linen robe. There is again one of those illuminating, revealing sentences: 'The fine linen' of the Bride's robe for the great marriage 'is the righteous deeds of the saints' (19:8). Literally—'what makes righteous', the '*dikaiōmata*'. Of Zacharia and Elizabeth, Luke says that they were 'walking in all the commandments and ordinances (*dikaiōmata*) of the Lord' (1:6). The *dikaiōmata* of the saints are the fabric from which the robe of the Bride is made, as well as the garments of the warriors.

Here again emphasis is given to the important contribution that must come *from man* if the redeeming deed of the Lamb is to be truly beneficial. These three descriptions together (17:14; 19:8; 19:14) allow one to divine between the lines of the Apocalypse a continuous development. Again we notice an enhancement in the existence of Christians in the other world. They have produced the wedding garment; the word 'linen', especially, reminds us of the lengthy and laborious processes necessary for the production of linen. And they ride on white horses. The horse, in the imagery of myths and fairy tales, is related to intelligence. On the opening of the first four seals, at first the pure light of thinking appears as a white horse, then thinking is clouded by the impact of emotions—the red horse, then taken over by the power of gravity, concerned only with weights and measures—the black horse, and finally thinking that has become materialistic is dominated by the power of death itself—the pale horse. Man's power of feeling is to be permeated by Christ—the New Song, but his power of thinking and willing are not to be left out of this process. His intelligence, too, more and more in danger of falling into mechanical, dead thinking must be redeemed through being spiritualized. This is of decisive importance for mankind's future on earth. Unless the faculty of cognition is led towards the supersensible, mankind will fall into barbarism in spite of all the intellectual refinement. John's vision of the white rider indicates that Christ at His coming again will be borne by the power of spiritualized thinking. Knowledge of the spirit, in the sense of the Holy Spirit, wields the powerful sword of the Logos. As there is an 'eternal feminine' so there is also an 'eternal masculine'. Both should serve the Christ.

In the following chapter we see the excarnated souls in a last stage of advancement. The promise at the end of the letters begins to be fulfilled: 'I will grant him to sit with me on my throne' (3:21). As in the great vision of the throne in the fourth chapter, the seer lets us follow in his words the gradual development of the vision: first the 'thrones'; then figures appear which take their seats on the thrones; finally they can be recognised for what they really are—the souls of Christian martyrs. It is of importance that here, once more, as in the beginning of the whole series of pictures, the word '*psychai*', 'souls', is used (6:9 and 20:4). This series of pictures began with the souls 'under the altar'; then there are those robed in white with palms in their hands, then the harp players and singers of the New Song, then the riders on white horses. And now at the end once more the word 'souls' is used with emphasis. The resurrection of the body on the Last Day has not yet happened. Here the excarnated souls are counted 'blessed' because they share in the 'first resurrection' (20:6). But this is still the preliminary step, 'the life though one dies', the overcoming of the 'second death' which would darken the soul after death. The 'first death' (not expressly so called, but a term arising from the expression 'second death'), the death of the body, can be overcome only by reaching the final goal of the 'second resurrection' (again, not expressly so named, but arising from the context). Still at the beginning of the twentieth chapter, death as the last enemy is not removed from power. The 'first resurrection', however, within soul existence (the result of the mystery on the Saturday of Holy Week when Christ brought light into the realm of the dead), already procures for the souls of the saints an ego-conscious and active existence in the other world. They *live and reign with Christ as kings* for a long time (20:4). They are privileged to serve Christ as priests (20:6). By distinguishing between 'poor souls' and 'saints' Christians have shown themselves aware of the fact that excarnated souls may go through very different conditions. Poor souls are those dead whose loss of the body is not made up for by spiritual riches. The saints are those who live in the light of the spirit and who are able from their blessed existence to send forth their help to men on earth. The Apocalypse gives an inkling of a future when the effective working of those who have died in Christ will become a very much more powerful factor in human existence.

Those souls who are active as kings and priests are seen seated on thrones and making judgments. In this respect the consistency of the apocalyptic description has been questioned; that these souls 'judge' conflicts with the scene of the Last Judgment following soon after, in which the Lord God is the only judge. Yet here again the visions should not be seen as contradictory as if they followed 'pragmatic' rules of precise logic. Both visions are right in themselves and they do not contradict each other. When the souls take their seats on the thrones and 'judgment is committed' to them, it means that just by being what they are they become a measure by which other souls can judge themselves. On beholding a more exalted humanity, some souls experience judgment. This judgment through looking at the wholly righteous ones is, then, only a preliminary stage of the Last Judgment. The picture of the thrones for the saints is metamorphosed into the powerful image of the 'great white throne' (20:11).

*

In between, however, there is still another vision that leads us for the last time to the *earth*. Some Christians are still living below in earthly incarnations. Once more the adversaries rear up in a last great effort. The armies of Gog and Magog appear 'like the sand of the sea' as one great mass. They march forth like something risen from the underworld, a strange sight in the light of day. 'They marched up over the broad earth and surrounded the camp of the saints and the beloved city' (20:9). The saints on earth do not cling to material existence, settled and enjoying their possessions. They have no settled abode, and live in a camp like soldiers. The puzzling expression, 'beloved city' again indicates the heavenly Jerusalem, which has been prepared and announced in various preliminary stages, and of which this intrusive prevision is no contradiction to the picture of the camp. But the attack of the enemies, it seems, is easily repulsed this time. The mighty dead apparently help from above. 'Fire came down from heaven' deciding the battle and bringing the spectre of Gog and Magog to an end. During the final phase the power of goodness has matured to become 'white magic'. The time of the triumphant adversaries is over, after long development and many set-backs.

Now follows the picture of the 'great white throne'. The One seated on the throne performs the great white magic; the world dematerializes beneath His gaze. 'From his presence earth and sky fled away, and no place was found for them' (20:11). Space disappears. Human beings alone are left. They have to stand before the countenance of the One who sits on the throne. This is foreshadowed in a scene from the sixth seal; those living on earth hide in caves calling to the mountains and rocks: 'Fall on us and hide us from the face of him who is seated on the throne' (6:16). It is a first impression of the fact that man feels the penetrating eyes of a divine countenance directed towards him. The desire to hide and be covered by mountains —what else could it mean but flight down into material existence in order to deaden the first hints of the foreboding of judgment? Rudolf Steiner once called materialism a phenomenon of fear.—After the material world has fled away it is no longer possible to evade being seen. Material things have disappeared, but the deeds done by man in that transitory world have not vanished with it. They are spiritually recorded. The 'books' are opened and men judged accordingly. Only then is death completely overthrown. As already in the fourth seal, here, too, the spiritual powers of Death and Hades appear like persons who bring about death and the darkening of souls after death. Then the realm of the resurrection appears in the heavenly Jerusalem where the New Heaven and the New Earth become one.

★

The sequence of pictures in John's Apocalypse unmistakably shows a development in mankind's ability to receive Christ. 'Development' is quite obvious if one compares 6:9 and 20:4 where at the beginning and the end of the great progressive transformation the word 'souls' ('*psychai*') is used. The progress is not described in continuity; it reveals itself in separate momentary glimpses. But behind the scenes of the individual pictures something happens. The *progress* in man's joining himself with Christ becomes evident intermittently, from picture to picture, in a continuous change of scene between earth and heaven. The whole series of pictures forms a harmonious unit if, through reincarnation, one sees each individual Christian included in these changes of scene and the related reciprocal effects of periods of incarnation on earth and of excarnation in heaven which go on until the Last Day. It is much easier to find room for the idea of reincarnation in the Apocalypse with its widely separated epochs than in the concentrated eschatological views gathered up into one picture which we considered in the previous chapter.

Here the question could be raised: *Is another descent into earth existence thinkable* after the descriptions of heavenly bliss as given, for example, in the seventh chapter where one of the elders answers for the apocalyptist the question: 'Who are these, clothed in white robes . . . ?'—is it imaginable after such an exalted position has been achieved? We have already mentioned that this wonderful description of serving 'him day and night within his temple' (7:15) which seems to indicate something final and insurpassable, does not exclude the other picture that the Lamb 'will guide' these saints (7:17). Certain pictorial elements contained in the hymn of bliss re-occur at the end of the description of the heavenly Jerusalem. In 7:15 it is said that 'he who sits upon the throne' will dwell (literally) *above* them. The Jerusalem chapter (21) says: 'Behold, the dwelling of God is with men'—(dwelling, '*skene*', the tent, 'the tabernacle' of the exodus through the desert, to Jewish ears reminiscent of the '*shekhina*', the indwelling presence of God). 'He will dwell with them' (21:3). In the seventh chapter, excarnated human beings appear in the realm of God, in 'his temple'. The heavenly Jerusalem has no temple (21:22). What had been on the one hand the temple in heaven and on the other the temple on earth in the era of the 'old heaven' and the 'old earth' have now become one in the New Jerusalem, which is itself both the heavenly and the earthly temple. The heavenly temple has become identical with the world of man, the human 'city'. The precise use of different prepositions in the text should not be overlooked. In 7:15 there is '*epi*' ('*skenōsei ep' autous*'). He dwells 'above' them. In the New Jerusalem, the '*epi*' is replaced by '*meta*'—'with'. The experience of the nearness of the divine is enhanced. Thus in the picture of the seventh chapter the author of the apocalypse leaves *further development* still open. The tender image of wiping away 'every tear from their eyes' (7:17) is also repeated. This is certainly not 'just the same thing again'. If this experience of reconciliation with all earthly suffering appears again in the New Jerusalem it is certainly in an enhanced form. 'It will be and already is' holds good here, too. There are experiences which typically re-occur, but on ever higher levels. So 'bliss' can also be *on different levels*.

Already in religious life on earth moments of profound bliss can occur. They give a foretaste of a future still far off. That they pass is no argument against the truth and value of such moments. They have to give way, however, to less happy conditions, which man has to pass through for his further maturation. Something similar might also be true of existence in the other world if it is looked at realistically. Release from a sick, pain-stricken body can bring about an experience of true bliss with the foretaste of an unrestricted existence; nevertheless, in the further progress after death during the retrospective life experiences, there can also be very painful phases which must be lived through, but which may in turn be followed by brighter phases. The blessedness felt by Christian souls in the other world which the Apocalypse describes does not exclude an earthly incarnation being undertaken once more. In the sense mentioned before of man not losing himself in repeated earth lives, but, according to his inner strength, becoming more and more like himself, shining through the outer sheaths of his nature ever more clearly, his Christ-likeness would not be lost either but become richer and more firmly established from incarnation to incarnation. One region after another of man's broadly and comprehensively designed being could thus be laid open for Christ. The next period after death would again bring to maturity in the spiritual world the fruits of new experiences on earth, and again lead to other forms of bliss. What the young Goethe so ingeniously expressed: the '*Ahnden nach ferneren, verhülltern Seligkeiten dieser Welt** (the divining of further still-veiled joys of this world)', might also be relevant to the developments in the world beyond.

In his book, *Reincarnation*†, Friedrich Rittelmeyer gives the anthroposophical representation of the life after death in the following way: 'Every soul bears irrevocably within it the spiritual forces which draw it upward because, in its deeper nature, it is from above. But its past earthly life determines how high, how swiftly, how consciously it can enter the higher, the highest worlds, which all lie open for it' (p. 32). 'By the forces which draw our soul after them, will it be known where it belongs, whether to lower or to higher regions of the cosmos. No brief words of external judgment are spoken, but one relationship of our being after another comes before us, until the soul is "purified"; that means, till everything in it which can no longer live in the higher air has died. So the soul is drawn higher and higher till it reaches the "heaven" to which it has destined itself in its earthly life' (pp. 31–2). This experience of heaven, however spiritual and full of blessing it may be, is still relative, its limits determined by the preceding life on earth. It is *not yet absolute and final*. In each case it is an 'already now' which is a foretaste of a final future 'it will be'. In order to grow and mature for this end, new impacts, such as can be experienced only by man incarnated on earth, might be needed to further this development.

Let us just take note *at which places* in the progress of the great Apocalyptic drama the visions are inserted which have as their content *the progressive development of the excarnated Christian souls*, the '*psychai*', in the higher world. Clearly these visions are ordered *in three groups*, and, moreover, in connection

* *Gedichte von einem polnischen Juden*, Frankfurter gelehrte Anzeigen, 1 Sept. 1772.

† The Christian Community, London, *c.* 1931 (undated).

with the great Apocalyptic rhythms of seven.

As the book of Genesis describes the creation of the world in the framework of the seven-day week, so the Apocalypse describes the whole course of time in seven epochs, progressing, as it were, in octaves. The prelude, the seven letters to the churches in Asia, is followed by the epoch of the opening of the seven *seals,* then the sequence of the sounding of the seven *trumpets*, and finally the pouring out of the seven *bowls of wrath*.

The Christian souls who are in the other world appear first of all before John's prophetic eye on the opening of the fifth *seal* (6:9), one might almost say as if in a 'beginners' stage of their afterdeath existence (the souls 'under the altar'), but thereafter in a strengthened kind of supersensible existence, 'in grand style', in the seventh chapter ('clothed in white robes') between the sixth and seventh seals (7:9). Then the eye turns again to the earth when the *trumpets* sound, and remains directed to the earth till the seventh trumpet has sounded. As its sound reverberates, the Christians in heaven are visible and audible once again. As those who have 'conquered the beast' (15:2), who have come out of the sphere of its power victorious, and 'learned' the New Song, standing now beside the sea of glass, they are the singers of the eschatological song of salvation, endowed with full power and ability to make music on the harps of God. This enhancement of supersensible power is the outcome of what has been suffered and achieved on earth during the epoch of the trumpets.

This leads to the pouring out of *the bowls of wrath*, which at first is described as a sequence of terrible catastrophes, even more extensive and destructive than the events connected with the trumpets. After the passing of this last sevenfold sequence, the Christians in heaven are revealed a final stage higher, as knights with white horses, working as priests and kings, seated on thrones.

It is obvious that *in each case* after the sequence of the events of the seals, the trumpets and the bowls of wrath, the Christians in heaven show an *increase* in their supersensible powers of working.

If one did not take reincarnation into account, then the martyrs described in the seventh chapter would have achieved *their* degree of Christianization with the heavenly bliss following their experiences during the epoch of the seals. They, then, would stop at that and would have only to wait for the Last Day. But with whatever might be *their* achievement, they would remain outside what Christians of a later period on earth—during the epoch of the trumpets—gained as still greater spiritual power. The realm of the beast described in chapter 13 (still in the sphere of the seventh trumpet) shows beyond doubt an increase of power compared with the manner in which evil worked on earth at the time of the seals. The evil of which the early martyrs became victims had not yet reached that level of intellectual refinement with which the realm of the Antichrist and its evil despotism is organized to perfection ('so that no one can buy or sell unless he has the mark . . . of the beast' . . . 'on the right hand or the forehead' (13:17,16)). The evil had not yet become mature enough to produce 'miracles' with ungodly magic. This also means, however, that through suffering and overcoming this more refined evil even *enhanced forces of good* can be brought forth, whereby the whole compass of the human being, the *humanum*, is expanded to embrace the spiritual. In this increase in stature the martyrs of the epoch of the seals would have no share if they had to remain at that stage of development which was then within their reach.

The same would again be true for the Christians in heaven who came from the epoch of the trumpets in comparison with those coming after them who had to undergo, in further world development, the trials of the bowls of wrath. Their spiritual knighthood, their royal priesthood and the fulfilment of their enthroning would not have come about without the confrontation with the world-annihilating catastrophes of the bowls of wrath.

A different picture arises if reincarnation is taken into account. Then *Christendom as a whole* would pass through all these epochs, participating in the various trials, but also sharing as a whole in the various possibilities of achievement. The individual would not have to finish up with the outcome of one earthly existence, and in one 'intervening state' wait for the Last Day. He would be included in the whole progressive development of mankind. The idea of an 'intervening state', whether spent in sleep or in expectation, even perhaps blissful expectation, is somewhat unsatisfactory. Without it, the process of 'becoming Christian' begun in one incarnation on earth may be seen as unfolding further through new earth experiences and new sojourns in heaven in a perfectly fulfilled, ever developing life with the gradual *transformation 'into his likeness from one degree of glory to another'*.

Also by Rudolf Frieling

Hidden Treasures in the Psalms

The Psalms of David rank with Homer, Dante, Shakespeare and Goethe as the great inspiring sources of European poetry. Much of the original inspiration and wisdom has, however, been lost in translation and by associations with outdated doctrine. Rudolf Frieling has a gift for uncovering these hidden treasures in the Psalms, and for presenting them afresh. His scholarly grasp of the original Hebrew language and his profound sense of the mystical and even occult significance of the sacred poetry makes these studies a unique guide to the most beautiful book of the Old Testament.

Christian Community Press, distributed by Floris Books, Edinburgh

Also by Rudolf Frieling

The Essence of Christianity

The question of the nature of Christianity is inseparable from that of the nature of man himself. Modern man feels this question weighing even more heavily upon his consciousness. 'What is man all about?' Rudolf Frieling surveys man's relationship with God and with evil before and after the coming of Christ. He traces the central significance of the coming of Christ in man's free development towards likeness with Christ.

The Metamorphosis of the Eucharist

The development of the Eucharist from the Last Supper through the early Christian era to its rebirth in the twentieth century.

Christian Community Press, distributed by Floris Books, Edinburgh

Christianity as Mystical Fact and the Mysteries of Antiquity

by Rudolf Steiner

This is one of Rudolf Steiner's earlier books, but its very condensed substance foreshadows the whole tenor of his life's work. He appears as the first man of the modern age to call attention to the supreme importance of the mysteries of antiquity and to speak of the 'Mystery of Golgotha' as the final consummation of the spiritual experience which they induced.

Steiner describes the character of mystery wisdom and then uses it to illumine mythology, the Greek sages, the Platonists, the Gospels and post-Christian writers such as Augustine. The result is a remarkable survey of man's inner development which forms both an introduction and a guide to the numerous lecture courses in which he developed the themes here handled.

The book is far from being concerned only with the past. It points also to the future, and the significance for the modern age of the ever-renewing Christ-Impulse.

Rudolf Steiner Press, London